Death
and
Dying
in the
Classroom:

Readings
for Reference

Death and Dying in the Classroom:

Readings for Reference

Edited by James L. Thomas

 ORYX PRESS
1984

Copyright © 1984 by
The Oryx Press
2214 North Central at Encanto
Phoenix, AZ 85004-1483

Published simultaneously in Canada

Library of Congress Cataloging in Publication Data
Main entry under title:

Death and dying in the classroom.

  Bibliography: p.
  Includes index.
  1. Children and death. 2. Terminally ill children—
Psychological aspects. 3. Death—Psychological aspects—
Study and teaching. I. Thomas, James L., 1945–   .
BF723.D3D43   1984   306'.9'071   83-43240
ISBN 0-89774-137-4

Contents

Preface

For far too many years the topic of death and dying has been considered by most educators to be a taboo subject, especially in elementary and secondary school settings. Although most children and young adults have experienced the death of a pet or relative, the school classroom has not been used as a forum for discussing this reality until recently.

One of the main reasons that classroom teachers and librarians have been reluctant to discuss this topic is that few have had the opportunity to participate in any formal courses. Preservice and inservice workshops have rarely dealt with death and dying. Only over the past few years have colleges of education and library science programs attempted to offer classes on the topic. As a result of this lack of formal preparation, teachers and librarians naturally have found it difficult to handle the questions that come from children and young adults. Yet most professionals who have worked with young people in the classroom for any length of time can verify that the subject is broached on a regular basis.

During the past few years there has been an increased awareness of death education as a suitable and necessary aspect of the school curriculum. What is to be gained from discussing this topic with children and young adults? What is the value of including this in the curriculum? The "experts" that support the necessity for dealing with death and dying in the classroom have convincingly taken the following stands:

Perhaps the greatest benefit of teaching taboo subject matter is that the taboo is automatically removed. By discussing death, its implied sacred and unclean character—along with the accompanying myths, stereotypes and invalid generalizations—are held open to examination and scrutiny. If taught properly, death education is very much concerned with life in the fullest sense of the word. It should enhance man's reverence for and joy of life by reducing his fear of death.[1]

Perhaps the most intriguing aspect of the challenge posed by the subject is its reconstructive nature. . . . Education in death and dying is an agent of great promise for balancing the curriculum and making it a more complete approximation of life. Ultimately it promises to add a richer appreciation for the value of existence.[2]

If you can begin to see death as an invisible, but friendly, companion on your life's journey—gently reminding you not to wait till tomorrow to do what you mean to do—then you can learn to *live* your life rather than simply passing through it.[3]

It is ironic that children bear witness to eighteen thousand deaths on television by the age of fourteen, yet are not allowed to see terminally ill parents and grandparents who may be cloistered in an antiseptic hospital or home for the aged.

Death should be an integral part of the education of the whole child. . . .

Children, so many of whom have fears about death, must have an opportunity in their families and their schools to express their concerns and to discuss them with others.[4]

The primary purposes of this book are to encourage educators to discuss this topic openly with their students and to provide a variety of approaches using classroom-tested activities. The book should also serve to fill a void in the literature. Educators have just recently through journal articles focused attention on this topic. This compilation reflects "the best" personal accounts by experienced educators and the ways they have creatively discussed death and dying with their students.

In the Introduction, the first article provides the reader with an overview of the feelings children express when confronted with death and what these should mean to the educator. In the companion article, the authors explore practical guidelines that should assist with helping the grieving, dying, or simply curious child in dealing with and understanding a loss or potential loss.

The three sections that follow reflect the subject areas that surfaced while the editor was researching the topic. In Section I, "Teachers' and Students' Perceptions," the articles establish a rationale for death education, explain how children from ages three through adolescence deal with the concept, examine what effects loss has on these age groups, and present pupils' perceptions that have emerged during research investigations and group counseling.

In "Instructional Methods," Section II, the articles relate specific problems in and methods for handling the terminally ill child in the classroom setting. This section is rich with ideas and approaches for either separate units on the topic or methods for integrating death and dying into other curriculum units. Section II concludes with suggested criteria for evaluating curriculum materials for grades K through 12.

The final section "Classroom Encounters/Personal Narratives" reveals a series of positive statements by students and teachers who have witnessed and learned from first person encounters with death. These articles address the difficult yet essential challenges of exploring, discussing, sharing, and mutually growing from their experiences.

The three appendices contain a listing of media—print and nonprint—suitable for children and young adults to read or view; a selective listing of organizations and associations that will supply information on death and dying; and finally, a questionnaire that might be used with children or young adults to stimulate discussion. The book concludes with a selective, annotated bibliography of sources for additional exploration and/or purchase.

James L. Thomas
Editor

REFERENCES

1. Daniel Leviton in Joanne Zazzaro, "Death Be Not Distorted," *Nation's Schools* 91 (5) (May 1973): 40.

2. John W. McLure, "Death Education," *Phi Delta Kappan* 55 (7) (March 1974): 485.

3. Joseph L. Braga and Laurie D. Braga, "Foreword," in *Death: The Final Stage of Growth*, by Elisabeth Kübler-Ross (Englewood Cliffs, NJ: Prentice Hall, 1975), p. x.

4. David Sadker, Myra Sadker, and Carol Crockett, "Death—A Fact of Life in Children's Literature," *Instructor* 85 (7) (March 1976): 75.

Contributors

Constance D. Berg is Counselor and Art Teacher at Northwestern Junior Senior High School, Good Hope, IL. She has been a registered art therapist since 1975 and has published in the fields of art education, art therapy, and counseling. "Helping Children Accept Death and Dying through Group Counseling" originally appeared in *Personnel and Guidance Journal* (November 1978, vol. 57, no. 8, pp. 169–72). Copyright © 1978 American Association for Counseling and Development. Reprinted with permission.

David W. Berg is Editor, *Thanatology Abstracts*. "Teaching about Death" is reprinted with permission from *Today's Education* (March 1973, vol. 62, no. 3, pp. 46–47).

Ellen Huntington Bryant teaches on a part-time basis at Tower Hill School in Wilmington, DE. She has experience as a director of publications and technical editor. "Teacher in Crisis: A Classmate Is Dying" is reprinted from *Elementary School Journal* (March 1978, vol. 78, no. 4, pp. 233–41). Reprinted with permission of the author and publisher. Copyright © 1978 by The University of Chicago Press.

Alta Fleming Butler is a member of the faculty, Professional Studies in Early Childhood Education, Wheelock College, Boston, MA. "Scratchy Is Dead" is reprinted from *Teacher* (February 1978, vol. 95, no. 6, pp. 67–68). Copyright © 1978 by Macmillan Professional Magazines. Used by permission of The Instructor Publications, Inc.

Toni Dahlgren is co-author with Iris Prager-Decker of the article "A Unit on Death for Primary Grades," reprinted with permission from *Health Education* (January–February 1979, vol. 10, no. 1, pp. 36–39).

George G. Daugherty teaches history and government at DeKalb High School, DeKalb, IL. "Teaching about Death" is reprinted with permission from *Today's Education* (March 1973, vol. 62, no. 3, pp. 46–47).

Ben E. Dickerson is Director of the Gerontology Program and Professor of Sociology, Baylor University, Waco, TX. "Puppet Life and Death Education" is reprinted with permission from *The Clearing House*, Vol. 51, No. 9, May 1978, pages 458–459, a publication of the Helen Dwight Reid Educational Foundation.

David Ellis is Senior Psychologist, The Devereux Foundation, Devon, PA. "Reactions of Pupils and Teachers to Death in the Classroom" is reprinted from *School Counselor* (March 1978, vol. 25, no. 4, pp. 228–35). Copyright © 1978 American Association for Counseling and Development. Reprinted with permission.

Delphie J. Fredlund is Professor Emeritus of Maternal and Child Health, School of Public Health, University of Minnesota, Minneapolis, MN. "Children and Death from the School Setting Viewpoint" is reprinted with permission from *The Journal of School Health* (November 1977, vol. 47, no. 9, pp. 533–37). Copyright © 1977 American School Health Association, Kent, Ohio 44240.

Marianne (Everett) Gideon wrote "Criteria for Evaluating Curriculum Materials in Death Education from Grades K–12," *Death Education* (Summer 1977, vol. 1, no. 2, pp. 235–39). Reprinted with permission of Hemisphere Publishing Corporation.

Rose Grobstein is Chief Pediatric Social Worker, Stanford University Medical Center, Stanford, CA. She also lectures at Stanford Medical School and the University of California—Berkeley. "School Management of the Seriously Ill Child'' is reprinted with permission from *The Journal of School Health* (May 1974, vol. 44, no. 5, pp. 250–54). Copyright © 1974 American School Health Association, Kent, Ohio 44240.

David M. Kaplan is Professor Emeritus, Stanford Medical School, Stanford, CA. "School Management of the Seriously Ill Child'' is reprinted with permission from *The Journal of School Health* (May 1974, vol. 44, no. 5, pp. 250–54). Copyright © 1974 American School Health Association, Kent, Ohio 44240.

Charles R. Keith is Associate Professor of Psychiatry, Duke University Medical Center, Durham, NC. "Reactions of Pupils and Teachers to Death in the Classroom'' is reprinted from *School Counselor* (March 1978, vol. 25, no. 4, pp. 228–35). Copyright © 1978 American Association for Counseling and Development. Reprinted with permission.

Don Knowles is Professor, Psychological Foundations in Education, University of Victoria, Victoria, BC, Canada, and co-author of *But Won't Granny Need Her Socks?* (Kendall Hunt, 1983). "Understanding Children's Concerns about Death and Dying'' and "Helping Children Deal with Death Concerns'' are reprinted by permission of the *B.C. Journal of Special Education* (Spring 1981, vol. 5, no. 1, pp. 33–40; pp. 41–48).

Martin J. Lubetsky, MD, is Resident in Psychiatry, Sinai Hospital in Detroit, MI, and began a Child Psychiatry Fellowship at Western Psychiatric Institute and Clinics, Pittsburgh, PA, in July 1984. "When a Student Dies. . . .'' by Michelle S. Lubetsky with Martin J. Lubetsky is reprinted from *Teaching Exceptional Children* (Fall 1982, vol. 15, no. 1, pp. 27–28). Copyright © 1982 by The Council for Exceptional Children. Reprinted with permission.

Michelle S. Lubetsky is a teacher of trainable mentally impaired adolescents in Berkley, MI. She also teaches dance for handicapped students in Birmingham, MI. She was the recipient of the Teacher of the Year Award for the Oakland County Association for Retarded Citizens in 1981. "When a Student Dies. . . .'' by Michelle S. Lubetsky with Martin J. Lubestky is reprinted from *Teaching Children* (Fall 1982, vol. 15, no. 1, pp. 27–28). Copyright © 1982 by The Council for Exceptional Children. Reprinted with permission.

Molly Oakley is a second grade teacher at Central School in Cambridge, NY. "The Year We Had Aaron''

in *The Most Enabling Environment* (Wheaton, MD: Association for Childhood Education International 1979, pp. 59–62) is reprinted by permission of the author and the Association for Childhood Education International. Copyright © 1979 by the Association, 11141 Georgia Ave., Suite 200, Wheaton, MD 20902.

Estelle Parness is now deceased. She was the author of "Effects of Experiences with Loss and Death among Preschool Children,'' which originally appeared in *Children Today* (November–December 1975, vol. 4, no. 6, pp. 2–7).

Iris Prager-Decker is Assistant Professor of Health Education, George Mason University, Fairfax, VA. "A Unit on Death for Primary Grades'' is reprinted with permission from *Health Education* (January-February 1979, vol. 10, no. 1, pp. 36–39).

Nancy Reeves has her MA in counseling psychology and has worked extensively with bereaved parents and grieving and dying children for six years. She has a private counseling practice, is Grief Consultant to Queen Alexandra Children's Hospital, teaches a course on grieving at the University of Victoria, Victoria, BC, Canada, and conducts workshops and courses throughout Canada. "Understanding Children's Concerns about Death and Dying'' and "Helping Children Deal with Death Concerns'' are reprinted with permission of the *B.C. Journal of Special Education* (Spring 1981, vol. 5, no. 1, pp. 33–40; pp. 41–48).

Nina Ribak Rosenthal is Associate Professor, California State College—Stanislaus, Turlock, CA. and is author of "Death Education: Help or Hurt?'' First printed in *The Clearing House,* (Vol. 53, January 1980, pages 224–226), a publication of the Helen Dwight Reid Educational Foundation.

Margaret E. Rucker is a retired Associate Professor of Home Economics, Stephen F. Austin State University, Nacogdoches, TX. "Puppet Life and Death Education'' is reprinted with permission from *The Clearing House,* Vol. 51, No. 9, May 1978, pages 458–459, a publication of the Helen Dwight Reid Educational Foundation.

Edwin S. Schneidman is Professor of Thanatology. University of California—Los Angeles. He compiled "You & Death: A Psychology Today Questionnaire.'' The questionnaire is reprinted with permission of the author from *Psychology Today* (August 1970, pp. 67–70). Copyright © 1970 by Edwin S. Schneidman.

Introduction

Understanding Children's Concerns about Death and Dying

by Don Knowles and Nancy Reeves

Much as we might wish to protect children from the frightening and awesome concerns about death, their experiences with life will inevitably lead them to encounter death. These encounters can be softened, and even become the basis of important, constructive development, if children have the support of understanding adults and have experienced situations which prepare them to view death as a naturally occurring event. Particularly since the pioneering study of Kübler-Ross (1969), considerable effort has been made to learn more about children's understanding of death and to develop guidelines which will help adults respond effectively to children's questions and concerns.

This article is concerned with the meanings and feelings that children have about death. A companion article [Helping Children Deal with Death Concerns] presents guidelines for teachers and other adults who are important to a child when questions about death arise or when a death occurs close to the child. Our ideas have developed from a series of workshops and consultations with teachers and parents throughout the province.

Developmental differences seem to be based on two important characteristics of children's thought: the capacity to create order out of disorder and the egocentrism of considering oneself to be the center of other people's activities.

Struggles to create order out of disorder lead children to place their own personal meanings on information or, in an area of silence or withholding of information, to develop their own explanations. For example, after a swimming lesson a young boy commented that he had fun and had "only drowned twice." Further discussion led his dad to ask about what happened after the drowning, to which the boy responded, "Then I came up again." His personal assignment of meaning to "drown" was quite unique and easier to accept than the conventional definition. It was also important for those talking to him to be aware of his meanings. LeShan (1976) reported the more disturbing example of a seven year old boy who was "spared" the information that a baby brother who had died at birth had been cremated. He was too shy to ask and within a few weeks:

> . . . began to feel afraid of going to school. He was afraid of the dark and wanted a light on in his room all night. He began to be afraid of opening a closet door or opening a dresser drawer . . . (eventually) Allen asked what had been done with the baby's body, and his father told him about burial and cremation. Allen said, "I thought the baby was somewhere in the house." (p. 15)

Clearly the strategy of remaining silent, in the interests of protecting children, does not ensure that a vacuum of information will persist. Further, the unique constructions of the child are important for adults to attempt to understand if communication about these important ideas is to take place.

The second characteristic, that of egocentrism, has been well documented by the work of Jean Piaget in other content areas. The young child tends to see events taking place for his or her benefit, such as a lake being "placed" close to a highway so that he will have easy access for swimming, and events being caused by his or her actions, such as a sailboat moving through the water because the child wishes to be conveyed somewhere. In trying to understand death and dying, the child shows similar characteristics. There may be some guilt about angry wishes in some way causing a person's death. In fact, this tendency may be reinforced by such parental warnings as "be quiet because grandpa is sick." On the other hand, an initial reaction to news of a death may appear to be unfeeling selfishness. For example, Rudolph (1978) quoted the following conversation involving a preschool child:

> "Granny, will you die?"
> "Yes, I'll die."
> "Will they bury you in a hole?"
> "Yes, they will bury me."
> "Deep?"
> "Deep."
> "That's when I'll be able to use your sewing machine." (p. 83)

Thus, this egocentristic characteristic is shown in a concern about personal well-being or in an assumption of blame, and resulting guilt. It is also evidenced in the child's wish to be in control and the resulting frustration when this control is removed by death or as part of the bereavement. For example, adults may make decisions about where the child stays or whether or not he continues in a school program in the interests of looking after him or her but with the result of further removing a sense of control from the child.

A somewhat different form of egocentrism typically is shown in later childhood and adolescence. One form is an assumption of a "personal fable" which arises in response to the many changes occurring to the adolescent's body, social world, and values. The adolescent is led to conclude that unique forces are operating in his or her life. Protests, such as "You don't know how it feels," are examples of this assumption. Adolescent reactions to death and dying may be characterized by an easy acceptance or relatively unemotional response due to the perception that death will not affect him or her because of this personal uniqueness. Similarly, various behaviors such as careless driving and "death-defying" stunts may be based primarily on the assumption that dying is something that affects other people.

A somewhat related form of adolescent egocentrism has been called the "imaginary audience" by David Elkind (1974). Because of increased self concern, the adolescent may come to assume that others are as interested in personal characteristics of the adolescent, such as complexion or clothing, as the adolescent is himself or herself. Reactions to death may have as a central focus what others will say about the adolescent, especially about changes which may lead to perceived differences. Hostler (1978) described the difficulty that medical staff had in explaining treatment plans to a fourteen year old boy with leukemia.

> When by the end of the week staff concerns are unchanged, the resident is frustrated and suggests that the patient may be retarded. After a case conference, house staff and nursing staff begin to understand the nature of Mike's denial. His only communication relative to his hospitalization is the stress over acne, possible weight gain, and what his school mates will think of his tracks of intravenous sites. (p. 22)

This emphasis on self concern, if not understood, can become the basis of strain between the adolescent and adults at a crucial time, such as when news of a death has been received, when support and sharing between them is particularly important.

These two developmental themes, egocentrism and creating order out of disorder, underlie specific characteristics which have been observed about children's understanding of death. Some of these specific characteristics are described in Table 1.

Table 1
Some Developmental Characteristics of Children's
Understanding of Death

AGE LEVEL	CHARACTERISTIC OF DEATH CONCEPT			
	REVERSIBILITY	FEAR/ANXIETY	BIOLOGICAL FUNCTIONING	BASIC UNDERSTANDING
EARLY CHILDHOOD (3–6 years)	death is gradual, may be reversed	brief, recurrent fear of abandonment, guilt	concern about hunger, warmth of dead person	magical
MIDDLE CHILDHOOD (6–10 years)	death is final and irreversible	increase in fear (8–9 years) may personify death	dead can see, hear, receive messages	specific and concrete
ADOLESCENCE	death is final, irreversible and universal	anxiety and denial about own death, goals interfered with	cessation of functioning understood	universal but remote

Young children seem to assume that death is a reversible process (''take them to the emergency room and get them doctored up'') so their fears and concerns are different than those of older children. Typically, at about 5 years of age there is great curiosity and a series of penetrating questions which most adults find somewhat unsettling. By age eight or nine years, most children understand that death is irreversible and may show through questions, sleep disturbances, and general unsettledness that their fear of death has increased. In adolescence there may be a more generalized anxiety about death, and associated denial, apparently as a result of having become capable of contemplating the deep meanings of one's own death. Further information about these developmental characteristics is provided in such articles as those by Hostler (1978), Reeves and Knowles (1979), and Weininger (1979).

In the early period, normally three to six years, children may play happily during mourning periods then show brief but intense concerns particularly about the physical changes accompanying death. A five year old, for example, was concerned that his grandmother should be buried with warm socks on to keep her comfortable. Another young child performed an elaborate burial for his dog, including the placement of two cans of dog food in the grave. Children in this early period may also confuse wishes with behavior, concluding that an angry or jealous thought about a sibling, parent, or grandparent may be associated with the death. Similarly, they may come to doubt the security of the lives of other people around them and develop undue concerns about abandonment.

During middle childhood, involvement in mourning activities is important to provide appropriately concrete information about what is happening. The religious beliefs and orientation of the family may gain new importance to children at this time. Experiences which may be associated with death, such as hospitalization, should be clearly explained to reduce the possibility that misunderstanding may unduly accelerate fears about dying.

In adolescence, concern may be primarily about how others react to a mourning person. A dying or sick adolescent may be very concerned about the side effects of the disease or treatment on his physical body, such as weight gain or loss of hair. In response to the death of an age-mate, adolescents may glorify the event or the person, perhaps in an attempt to deal with the anxiety associated with the reminder of their own mortality. An initial reaction to the death of a parent or teacher may be to question the implications on goals that are being developed. For example, plans for vocational training may be interfered with as a result of parental death.

These developmental characteristics are affected, of course, by the unique experiences each individual encounters. For example, religious teachings may affect the anxiety associated with death. Portrayals of death in the popular media, such as television, may aid or interfere with the development of reasonable understandings of death. In contrast to earlier portrayals of death as having only superficial implications, recent television programs have addressed the feelings and other reactions shown by survivors. The effect on each individual child of these experiences can be understood only by attending to that child. One clear implication of our work has been to expect children to have concerns and reactions that are different from those of adults but to be aware of making broad assumptions about how an individual child will react.

Most children will have developed their own understandings of death by the time they experience the death of a close family member or school friend. This understanding may show some of the characteristics of concreteness, egocentrism, and magical thinking. An initial task of adults interested in providing appropriate support to a child experiencing a death is to appreciate this understanding and its related concerns. Appropriate explanations and other reactions by the adult will then be possible. Guidelines for teachers and parents are provided in our companion article.

REFERENCES

Elkind, D. *Children and adolescents*. Toronto: Oxford University Press, 1974.

Hostler, S. The development of the child's concepts of death. In O.J.Z. Sahler (Ed.), *The Child and death*. Saint Louis: Mosby, 1978.

Ipswitch, E. *Scott was here*. New York: Dell, 1979.

Kübler-Ross, E. *On death and dying*. New York: Macmillan, 1969.

LeShan, E. *Learning to say goodbye: What to do when a parent dies*. New York: Macmillan, 1976.

McCullough, C. *Tim*. New York: Popular Library, 1974.

Reeves, N., & Knowles, D. Death concerns of children and adolescents. *B. C. Counsellor*, 1979. *1*, 5–14.

Rudolph, M. *Should the children know?* New York: Schocken Books, 1978.

Weininger, O. Young children's concepts of dying and dead. *Psychological Reports*, 1979, *44*, 395–407.

Helping Children Deal with Death Concerns

by Nancy Reeves and Don Knowles

"What is dead?"
"How will he eat when he's in the ground?"
"Why did she leave me?"
"Will you die?"
"What happens after you die?"

Any adult who spends much time with children has been asked these or similar questions. Many adults find the answers difficult. In numerous workshops conducted in British Columbia for parents, teachers, counsellors, and physical and mental health care practitioners the authors repeatedly encountered the following adult concerns:

"I don't want to say the wrong thing and make the hurt worse."
"I heard about Lucy's mother's death from another class member. Since Lucy didn't tell me herself I am uncertain whether to introduce the topic."
"He's so young! What can I say that he will understand?"
"I'm afraid if the parents hear that we've discussed death in the classroom they'll accuse me of pushing religious beliefs."
"I haven't sorted out my own thoughts and feelings about death. How can I help my students?"

This article will present practical guidelines for responses to the concerns listed above. To be maximally helpful to a grieving or dying child or a child curious about death an adult should have an awareness and understanding of four areas. These include:

1. own feelings and attitudes about death,
2. how children develop an understanding of death,
3. general stages and physiological and psychological symptoms of dying and grieving, and
4. general and specific helping behaviors.

The first and fourth areas are covered in this article. The third area can be found in numerous books and articles (Kübler-Ross, 1969; Reeves and Knowles, 1979). Chil-dren's understanding of death has been described in the preceding article by the authors.

DEATH AWARENESS

Without an examination of our own feelings and attitudes about death we are likely to misunderstand a child's questions and concerns or to make an incorrect assumption of how to help. A deep, extensive self-examination is unnecessary. If we know the origin of some of our feelings and attitudes and are able to separate our reactions from those of the child we are trying to help, we will have a greater chance of being effective.

At any one time we view "death" as either positive, negative, or neutral. Our orientation to death is dependent both on our present and past experiences with this topic. A person who sees death as positive will describe it as natural, welcoming, a release, gone to his reward. Words and phrases such as unfair, scary, tragic, cut off in his prime, describe a negative orientation. A neutral orientation uses terms as the end, deceased, finished. If our feelings and attitudes about death are flexible we will be able to switch orientations to be appropriate to a specific situation. For example, a bedridden terminally ill child, who is experiencing a lot of pain, would not be helped by being told how unfair it is that a child has to die, when he or she talks about the peace death will bring.

Our past experiences with death may have made us flexible or rigid in our orientation to death and loss. A child who loses a parent through death, separation, or divorce neither is automatically scarred for life nor necessarily sees all loss as negative. The child whose parent dies may develop a rigid orientation to death if he is not allowed to grieve in his own manner with the support of accepting, understanding adults. By rigid we mean that the individual sees death at all times in one way and cannot understand or believe that others would view it differently. Living with a rigid orientation is restrictive for it prevents individuals from developing a range of coping skills. Our present experiences also affect our orientations, changing our feelings and attitudes often.

By listening to the words others use when talking about death or loss we gain insight to their orientation and may become aware of what help would be useful. A child might ask about death in a neutral way, out of curiosity, "Is the squirrel dead?" An adult may answer with a negative orientation, "Yes, he is. The poor little thing, isn't that sad?" The child, picking up his cue from the adult may think he was wrong to feel curiosity rather than sorrow. An adult, responding to the same question with a positive orientation, "The little squirrel has gone to his reward and is at peace," also misses providing the child with the information he asked for. The child has asked the adult to confirm a fact and may or may not have other questions when he is told that, "Yes, the squirrel is dead."

Some of the words we use to describe death are called "euphemisms." The Merriam-Webster Dictionary defines euphemism as "the substitution of a pleasant expression for one offensive or unpleasant." Phrases such as "passed away" and "gone to meet his Maker" are often used to soften the fact instead of using the more direct "dead or died." The current fad of "death awareness and education" carries some judgments about euphemisms. Some proponents say "call a spade a spade, always use the straight terms." Euphemisms are viewed as a cop-out. However, this judgment seems rigid and does not consider the many reasons we use euphemisms.

Using direct words, dead, died, is helpful because they will not be misinterpreted. Euphemisms such as "gone" and "long sleep" may confuse and, if taken literally, frighten a child. If euphemisms are used exclusively for a long period of time they could be a way of denying the fact of a death and therefore be unhealthy. Denial is, however, healthy and necessary for some part of a grieving process. During that time euphemisms may be needed as a way of making the loss more manageable. Also, people close to death may use words like "passing away" not as a method of avoiding but because that was the phrase used in their youth. Dying people often revert to a native tongue periodically or reminisce and use familiar words from the past. Such word choice is a normal experience. In times of stress we often long for "the good old days."

The second area of self-examination involves our fears and concerns of the process of dying or grieving. It is extremely difficult to help someone unless we are aware of that person's concerns. With an emotionally laden topic such as death it is easy to think that our concerns are identical to those around us but that is often an incorrect assumption. For example, the knowledge that a grade one child has been killed by a drunk driver will produce different reactions in everyone involved. The child's teacher may feel furious; classmates may feel bewildered and sad that their friend isn't there to play.

In workshops we ask participants to describe the worst possible personal death they can imagine. The responses have been diverse: drowning, mauled by a grizzly bear, plane crash, torture, prolonged illness, etc. The specific deaths are unique to the individual but, by looking more closely, a few recurrent elements can be found. These common fears about grieving or dying include: being out of control, being isolated or alone, emotional or physical pain, being a burden to others, the unknown, being pitied or viewed as worthless. A major fear for one person might be of little concern for another. Contemplating a prolonged terminal illness, Janice might feel that pain would be the worst aspect, Chris might fear being a burden to his family. By listening carefully to children we can often hear the fears they have and therefore gain clues as to how we can be most helpful.

HELPING SKILLS

Self Awareness

We have examined two ways to clarify our views of death in general. Awareness of our reactions to a specific death is also important. The death of a student or teacher affects the whole school to some extent. If the staff members who are emotionally touched by the death have an opportunity to talk briefly about their reactions with their peers *before* interacting with their students they will accomplish two valuable goals. First, the staff members will likely feel more supported in their own grieving; second, as a team they will be able to work out a plan of action for presenting the news to the students and dealing with the subsequent reactions.

Children learn how to grieve by watching the significant adults in their lives. A teacher's expression of grief in class teaches the students that strong emotions are natural and that mourning does not have to be hidden away. Sharing reactions to loss helps us feel less alone.

Providing Information

We have been careful not to advocate a systematized death education program for children. Questions and concerns about death arise each school year after a death or because of some aspect of the curriculum. Times when the interest comes from the class are the most appropriate to provide information about stages and types of grieving and dying.

When a death occurs, students need to hear some facts or they will speculate and fantasize their own information. These fantasies are often more disturbing than the reality.

Inviting

A school counsellor told us that no one in her school had ever needed help with a death concern because no student or staff member had ever approached her on this subject. We were not surprised. Grieving people rarely directly reach out for assistance; they are preoccupied with their mourning, they may be afraid of being a burden or being seen as weak, and they may not realize how talking about their grieving can help them. It therefore rests on the teacher or counsellor to offer support. Statements like, ''I imagine this is a hard time for you, I'd sure like to talk about it if you want,'' or ''There's a lot of changes that happen in our minds and bodies when we grieve, if you'd like I can describe them to you,'' show the student your interest.

Checking Out

A common concern of teachers and counsellors is intruding on a grieving child, saying or doing the wrong thing. If you are unsure what would be helpful there are two courses you can take. The first is to ask. It is remarkable how many children, even preschoolers, know what help they need.

> Teacher: (*to grade four student*) ''John, I just heard your grandma died. I'd like to help if there's anything I can do.''
> John: ''I'm OK but sometimes I cry and can't stop.''
> Teacher: ''That seems to bother you, not being able to stop your tears.''
> John: ''I don't want the kids to watch me!''
> Teacher: ''OK, how about if when you start to cry you go down to the nurse's room where the kids won't see you. I can set that up for you or if you have any other ideas of what we can do we can talk about those.''
> John: ''I'd like to go to the nurse's room. Thanks.''

This brief conversation before class dealt with a concern that John might otherwise worry about all day. The teacher has also shown himself to be an ally, and John is more likely to approach him with other concerns or questions. If the teacher is aware of something that may affect a grieving student, he or she demonstrates respect and faith in the child by mentioning this and deciding with the child on a course of action. ''We're going to be talking about the death of Louis Riel today. How do you feel about being a part of the discussion?''

Sometimes asking a child directly what would be helpful is inappropriate. In these cases, an attempt should be made to offer help tentatively while watching the child's reaction. This tentativeness is especially effective with touching. There is nothing more intrusive than a hug that is unwanted, or more supportive than a hug that is. Touch a student gently and briefly on the arm. If the child wants more physical contact he or she will smile, lean towards you and may even reach out with their arms. The student who doesn't want physical contact will draw away.

Maintain Structure and Routine

A common fear of grieving children is that they will be seen as not coping well or that they will be treated differently than fellow students. A sensitive teacher is aware that a student will have more difficulty paying attention to schoolwork during the grieving process (Reeves & Knowles, 1979); the student also wants to be viewed as a functioning, useful part of the class. A balance must be found. The school routine can be an emotional anchor when homelife is strange and disrupted. For some children, jobs such as safety patrol or school monitor may be too much just after a loss, for others the positions provide a much needed affirmation of stability.

Grieving children are often worried by the changes a loss produces in their livestyles. Sometimes parents become slacker about rules—bedtimes, TV watching, eating behaviors. The child may react to these changes by testing many or all the limits in his or her life. The child needs the significant adults around him or her to maintain a firm, caring structure because the child then knows he or she has a place; the world is more understandable and safe. With no limits the world is chaotic and frightening.

Listening

We are including listening as a specific helping skill even though it may seem obvious. If, as adults, we are nervous when approached by a child with a death concern we may attempt to deal with our anxiety by talking a lot. We can easily overwhelm a child with information or lose his interest by answering more than he wants.

By listening in an accepting manner to a child's feelings and experiences and responding by demonstrating our understanding of what the child is saying, we show caring and support, help the child clarify and deal with concerns, and heighten the chances that the child will speak about the central issues.

When a child presents us with a question, we need to determine what is really being asked. It is easy to make assumptions. A child asked, ''Where did I come from?'' The parent, who had been waiting for this question for years replied with a well thought out explanation of sex and its consequences. The child sat a little impatiently through all this and then rephrased his question, ''John says he came from Ottawa before moving here, where did I come from?'' Such responses to children's questions as, ''Can you tell me some more about your question and I'll try to answer the best I can?'' or even initially putting the question back to the child, ''Can you tell me what you think about that?'' may provide specific information about a child's concerns and needs. Responding to the feelings of the child that are perceived may accomplish the same purpose: ''Sounds like you're feeling kinda confused about what will happen at the funeral.''

Sometimes a child's concerns are dealt with very quickly. Other times a discussion with a child about death may be full of silences as he or she mulls over questions and answers. Hurrying a child will cause him or her to withdraw but we may need to say at times, ''It seems like there's more to talk about and I have to leave in ten minutes. I'd like to get together again tomorrow.'' When a child is aware that we will listen respectfully and non-judgmentally he or she will bring concerns to us as they arise.

Rituals

The more children we hear about or work with around death issues the more we see some kind of ritual or ceremony as important. A ritual provides among other things:

1. a concrete indication that the death is real,
2. a demonstration of how others feel about the death,
3. a way of saying goodbye to the dead one and to the relationship, and
4. a reaffirmation and strengthening of the survivors' emotional bonds.

In order to accomplish the above objectives a ritual *must* be meaningful to those involved. Gettting dressed up in uncomfortable clothes, being shushed and made to sit for ages on hard seats to listen to an incomprehensible lecture provides no comfort. If a funeral or other cultural ritual is seen as meaningful to the parents it can become meaningful to the child. Children four years old and under will likely become bored and fidgety and will probably prefer to spend the time at a friend's house. They need to know the reason for the ritual, what will occur, how long it will take, and if possible be taken to the location beforehand so they have some familiarity. If an adult friend of the child can attend to quietly answer questions during the ceremony or take him or her to the toilet or outside as needed the experience can be a good one for the child. Being included with the adults is important.

In addition to or instead of the traditional cultural rituals, other ceremonies may be needed. When a student was killed in a car accident the school principal called assembly the next morning. He and some of the teachers spoke about the loss and then the students were dismissed to class. A student delegation came to the principal and said the assembly hadn't been enough for them. Attendance was compulsory and it was organized and controlled by staff. The students wanted their own meeting after school when only those really interested would attend. Only students would be allowed. The principal agreed and the students made the announcement on the PA system. The whole school turned out.

We can encourage and support child initiated rituals. We may invite rituals, ''The class guinea pig is dead, what shall we do with him?'', or if we are dealing with an individual grieving child, ''You told me you wished you could tell Grandma some things before she died. I know you like writing poems, how about writing one in honor of Grandma?''

A family ritual can bring the members closer together. Most families have some kind of ritual already operating. Saturday may be set aside for family activities, dinner may be the time the family members talk about their day and raise interests and concerns, bedtime may be kept for the whole family to snuggle together for awhile. These rituals provide a wonderful opportunity to talk about a death because the children understand what the time is for and view it as a normal continuing event. On the family hike a parent can say, ''Let's remember Grandpa today as we're walking and see if there's anything we can find that he would have enjoyed.'' The pretty stones, leaves, and feathers that the family collects may be placed on his grave or taken home. During the hike the conversation can be an easy, non-threatening way for the children to say goodbye. ''Boy, I bet he'd like this feather. He knew so much about birds. I'm sad 'cause I won't be able to ask him questions anymore.''

Grieving is natural and takes many forms. By being receptive to the children around us we can become aware of their needs and how we can help.

REFERENCES

Kübler-Ross, E. *On death and dying*. New York: Macmillan, 1969.
Reeves, N., & Knowles, D. Death concerns of children and adolescents. *B. C. Counsellor*, 1979, 1, 5-14.

Section I
Teachers' and Students'
Perceptions

Death Education: Help or Hurt?

NINA RIBAK ROSENTHAL

A first grade teacher reads a story about a pet that died. As a result, one of her students vividly describes seeing his dog die after being hit by a car. The student continues talking about his pet and becomes more and more upset until he begins to sob uncontrollably. The teacher, not prepared for such a reaction, does not know what to say or to do.

An eighth grade teacher shows a filmstrip about death and dying. After class, a student seeks out the teacher and discusses her mother's terminal illness and her own suicidal thoughts. The teacher becomes frightened and cannot respond.

A high school teacher tries to integrate death into a history lesson and, without preparing the students, presents a lesson comparing American burial practices in colonial times to practices in modern times. In her words, "Most of the students were upset; some were downright angry. One male student, who came to class looking happy, suddenly became 'ill' and asked to be excused." This teacher spent the weekend concerned about her students' reactions.

Just a decade or two ago, the idea of discussing death in a junior or senior high school seemed totally inappropriate, even absurd. Today, however, not only is teaching about death seen as appropriate; it is the "in" thing to do. Popular magazines (*Psychology Today, Newsweek, Time*), as well as educational journals (*English Journal, Journal of School Health, Learning, Science Teacher, Teacher, Today's Education*), have reported on the effects of death and dying courses and on the ways in which teachers integrate the subject of death and dying into their classroom (2), (3), (4), (6), (8), (9), (12), (13). Recognizing the increased marketability of resource materials in this area, publishers have increased their production of books, curriculum guides, audio cassettes, filmstrips, films, and prepackaged programs to help novice death educators teach students about death (5), (10).

As a result of the emphasis on the positive results of death and dying courses, the proliferation of materials, and the increased popularity of the subject matter, teachers seem to be jumping on the death bandwagon by offering full-length or mini-courses on death and dying. Some of these courses are being conducted by educators working with prepackaged death programs; other educators are taking a stab at death education with little knowledge and even less in the way of materials. Few school teachers have had training in this area and even fewer have been exposed to the problems and dangers associated with teaching about death and dying. Yet, little has been written describing the problems that can confront teachers who attempt to teach in this area and teachers are being encouraged to deal with death in the classroom without knowledge. In fact, on the cover of Stanford and Perry's (11) curriculum guide, one finds the statement, "With no special training you can teach death education as easily as you teach the basics." Surely, teachers must realize that it is not easy to teach the basics, and that when individuals teach about death, they can expect reactions somewhat different from those accompanying most academic subjects. Death arouses emotions; some students may get depressed; others may get angry; many will ask questions or make statements that can cause concern for the instructor. Death is not a topic about which people feel comfortable. On the contrary, death frequently makes one uncomfortable and this includes teachers as well as their students.

Death educators need to be ready to respond to students who tell them their personal feelings about death. Students may discuss the fact that they are having nightmares or that the course is making them depressed or feeling morbid. Some participants may begin to work on unresolved grief and go through feelings of guilt or sadness; some may cry in class; others may have no reactions or feel a great sense of relief that someone finally is talking about the things they often felt they could not say. Others may become frightened. In fact, Bailis and Kennedy (1) report that secondary students increased their fear of death and dying as a result of participating in a death education program.

What does all this mean? Do these feelings always occur? Does this mean that death education is not worthwhile and should be eliminated? The answer to each question is an emphatic NO. However, teachers must be made aware of the pitfalls and problems as well as the benefits and rewards involved in teaching about death.

By producing prepackaged programs and reporting only the positive effects of death education courses, the media seems to have glamorized courses on death and dying and thus may have encouraged poorly prepared teachers to use death as a dramatic way to gain their students' interest. However, along with this interest may come problems, problems for which these teachers are neither prepared for nor capable of handling. For example, in a graduate level death education class I conducted recently, a student approached me after class and described how depressed the class made her feel. She wanted to know if her reaction was a common one. When I informed her that her feelings were not unusual, she suggested that students should be prepared for this type of reaction. (Students were informed during the next class of the possibility and probability of such reactions.) After listening to the student, I suggested that she share her concerns with other members of the class. The following day, this student shared her thoughts and feelings and then proceeded to describe a present situation which included a great deal of grief. Although not grieving over a death, the student was in pain and expressed intense emotions. At times she cried, laughed, felt embarrassed or confused. The class and I responded with understanding and empathy and this student was able to clarify her thoughts and feelings in a therapeutic atmosphere.

My background as a counselor and as a counselor educator enabled me to feel comfortable and prepared for this situation. But most teachers do not have training in counseling and many individuals who have had training in counseling find it difficult to handle emotions associated with grief. Yet, the situation described above is not unusual and teachers who deal with death will be approached for help with death-related concerns. As Dan Leviton (7) states, "Undoubtedly, the death educator will be called upon to counsel in the areas of grief, personal dying and death, and/or suicide." Leviton further suggests

that while some death educators may be capable of both counseling and teaching, those who teach about death should learn when they need to refer students to other individuals. Since many psychiatrists, psychologists, and social workers may not be capable of handling death-related problems, however, death educators need to have a knowledge of not only when to refer but to whom they should refer their students (7).

Even the knowledge of capable helping persons is not enough. Teachers need more than knowledge of a referral before teaching about death. They need to be aware of their own attitudes, beliefs, and feelings about death. They need to know their reactions and feelings to various situations. Teachers need to ask themselves questions such as the following:

1. Why am I doing this? Is it a good way to attract attention? For whose benefit am I conducting the course?
2. How will I feel when students ask me difficult questions? Am I willing to share my viewpoints? Do I accept different points of view on topics like abortion, euthanasia, suicide, and religion, and can I teach both sides of these issues?
3. How will I feel if students seem quite upset when discussing death? Will I change the topic? Will I get depressed? What will my feelings be toward a student who directs hostility at me and at the course?
4. Will I be able to help a student who sobs uncontrollably? Will I be able to talk to a student whose mother is dying and the student expresses suicidal thoughts? Will I be able to listen to staff and faculty who want to talk about death and grief?

In addition to knowledge of self, teachers need factual knowledge on such diverse areas as suicide, euthanasia, funeral parlors, terminal illness, etc. They need to know various facts and theories associated with death and grief. The acquisition of such knowledge may be accomplished by reading books, attending seminars and lectures that deal with death, viewing films and filmstrips, and listening to some of the many cassette series available. Teachers need to have learned enough about the subject of death to feel competent to teach in this area. Furthermore, teachers might benefit from asking themselves questions such as the following:

1. Will I have enough knowledge to answer factual questions and have an understanding of what is happening in the subject area of death and dying? If I do not know the answers to ques-

tions, do I know the resources available to obtain these answers?

2. What are my objectives in teaching this course? Will I have the time to preview all materials that I plan to use and evaluate the worth of these materials? Do these materials help achieve my objectives?

3. Am I willing to plan and use alternate exercises for those students who do not want to participate in the experiences planned for that day?

4. Will I be willing to go to all field trip sites before taking my class there? Will I go to the cemetery, funeral home, etc. so that I know what the student may expect to encounter?

Still a third area of competence is needed for teaching about death. This area includes communication skills. Since death has been such a taboo topic, open and honest communication is essential. Such communication helps to desensitize students to anxiety-arousing items. While death educators should not be expected to counsel their students, they can and should be expected to demonstrate basic skills in listening and communicating about death. Before teaching about death, teachers should question themselves in the following ways:

1. Am I able to talk about death without using euphemisms? Can I respond to students in a genuine way without resorting to clichés and without being afraid that I might say the wrong thing?

2. Am I able to listen and not try to "cheer-up" the person? Can I respond empathetically by reflecting feelings or just remain silent if needed?

3. Can I somehow express the fact that I care? Am I willing to accept and able to accept the varying feelings associated with death and grief? Am I willing to share my own feelings?

4. Am I more concerned with what I might say rather than how I might help? Do I realize that sometimes a touch on the shoulder or hand of the student is sufficient in helping students?

Teachers, as well as their students, should be prepared for dealing with death and the many varied reactions accompanying grief. Teaching about death requires more than reading one "How To Do It" book. Self-awareness, information and communication skills are essential for death educators. Those who intend to work in this area should begin by answering the questions listed above, go to workshops, read books and articles, and/or participate in formalized training to obtain these essential competencies. It is hoped that teachers will take the necessary steps to insure that they help rather than hurt students who are dealing with death.

REFERENCES

1. Bailis, L. A., and Kennedy, W. R. "Effects of a Death Education Program upon Secondary School Students." *Journal of Educational Research* 71 (1977): 63-66.
2. Berg, D. W., and Daugherty, G. G. "Teaching about Death." *Today's Education* 62 (1973): 46-47.
3. Butler, A. F. "Scratchy Is Dead." *Teacher* 95 (1978): 67-68.
4. Fredlund, D. J. "Children and Death from the School Setting Viewpoint. *The Journal of School Health* 47 (1977): 533-537.
5. Griggs, S. A. "Annotated Bibliography of Books on Death, Dying and Bereavement." *School Counselor* 24 (1977): 362-371.
6. Hawkinson, J. "Teaching about Death." *Today's Education* 65 (1976): 41-42.
7. Leviton, D. "The Scope of Death Education." *Death Education* 1 (1977): 45-56.
8. Shiels, M. "Studying Death." *Newsweek,* March 14 (1977): 43.
9. Simon, S. B., and Goodman, J. "A Study of Death through the Celebration of Life." *Learning* 4 (1976): 70-74.
10. Stanford, G. "Methods and Materials for Death Education." *School Counselor* 24 (1977): 350-360.
11. Stanford, G., and Perry, D. *Death Out of the Closet: A Curriculum Guide to Living with Dying.* New York: Bantom, 1976.
12. Webb, A. I. "Death: The Last Taboo." *English Journal* 66 (1977): 55-56.
13. Yarber, W. L. "Death Education: A Living Issue." *Science Teacher* 43 (1976): 21-23.

Children and Death from the School Setting Viewpoint

by Delphie J. Fredlund

Most children are very interested in the subject of death, and at a very early age they begin to ask questions. As they grow older they gradually learn that death is something "you don't talk about," a response to the cues they have picked up from the adults around them. This trend needs to be reversed, and schools are in a significant position to contribute to a reversal.

Several years ago while on a sabbatical leave of absence, I worked three afternoons a week for an academic year with a group of 4½ to 5½ year old children in a university sponsored nursery school. Very early in the experience I became aware that these children were talking a lot about death, asking a lot of questions about death and acting out various aspects of death in their daily play. I became intrigued with their behavior and hypothesized that if they were talking and playing about death that much at school, they must also be doing these things at home, and I wondered how their parents coped with and felt about this behavior. I decided to do a study and I interviewed the mothers. As I had suspected, every one of the children had asked their parents many, many questions about death, including who it happened to, where the dead person or animal went, what he or it was doing now, when he or it would be back, how death happened, why it happened, and so forth. Some children had been curious about cemeteries and graves and caskets, and a few of them had asked theological questions about death. Almost all of the mothers expressed feelings of deep discomfort about their children's questions and play and said that they felt very inadequate about handling this aspect of their children's development. They all agreed that parents were primarily responsible, but over and over again they said, "Churches and schools must help."

Following is a discussion: (1) the development of a concept about death during the childhood years; (2) seriously ill and bereaved children in the school setting; (3) (very briefly) death education in the schools.

DEVELOPMENT OF A CONCEPT ABOUT DEATH

In the early part of this century most of the deaths occurred in the home, just as most of the funerals did, and also almost all of the births. Children were around—they heard the conversations, they saw the dying person as his disease progressed, they helped in the care, they knew that death was part of life in a very different way than our contemporary children do. At this time the education system also contributed a great deal to children's knowledge about death because many of the school books contained stories and poems about death and burial, often the death and burial of children. For example, one of the books commonly used in educating children 100 years ago, *McGuffey's Fifth Eclectic Reader*, included 57 poems, 27 of which clearly referred to death and dying.[1] Infant mortality was high, many children died from communicable and other diseases, medical technology was not nearly as far advanced as it now is, many mothers died in childbirth, men were involved in hazardous occupations and there were no safety codes. Many children actually were orphaned at an early age, and they regularly experienced the deaths of other children. There has always been a tendency for the writing of any period to reflect the personal and social conditions of the environment.

Many writers have contributed to the literature on how children develop an understanding about death, and there is general agreement that this understanding develops in an orderly sequence from a state of total unawareness in very early childhood through several stages to the point where death can be considered logically in terms of cause and outcome.

Under Three

Most children younger than three do not comprehend anything at all regarding death. They can and sometimes do experience grief in response to the loss of an essential person (i.e., the mother) but they are reacting to the separation aspect, and death as an understandable concept does not enter into their thinking.

From Three to Five

In the early part of this stage most children begin to accept that there is an all-powerful force in the universe that controls the workings of the world, and to which they must adjust.[2] If a child experiences a family death as early as three or four, the separation is still the most significant aspect, and his questions reflect this. "Where did he go?" "When will he come back?" "What is he doing?" These questions are very difficult to answer to the satisfaction of a very young child because of his limited frame of reference, and because he does not understand he may react with intense anger and experience severe rejection.

As children grow toward five they regard death as a departure, but they feel that it is reversible and that the dead person or animal will somehow return and go on just as usual, or that he is doing all the usual things when no one is looking, for example at night, or in the attic, or even in the grave they think that life continues. They also have considerable faith in their own omnipotence and their ability to make things happen, simply by wishing. Small children find it easy to wish death to people who interfere with their freedom but their threats of violence are meant to get the interferers out of their way, for the immediate present, so they can do as they please. The reversibility of death serves as a comforting protection to them.[3]

For four- or five-year-olds, immobility is the crucial factor about death, but of course it is reversible. They begin to accept that death happens to people but only when they are old. Most of them do not believe that they themselves will ever die or that children can die. Neither do most of them believe that they will ever get old; they can stretch their imaginations at age five to personal parenthood but to grandparenthood? That is much more difficult.

From Six to Nine

Children begin to believe that death is permanent as they grow toward six. This is associated with the development of the time sense; yesterday, next week, last month begin to have meaning. Many children become exceedingly anxious about death during this stage.[4] Perhaps this is the reason that Ilg and Ames said that children have their worst troubles about death when they are six years old.[5] Children are naturally boisterous and wild during this period and almost always consider death to be associated with violence. Most of them still

think of themselves as invincible during the early part of this stage, but as they approach eight they are beginning to accept that death is for everyone. They tend to regard death as a person and use many descriptive names. They associate death with darkness and feel that at night you have to step lively to keep out of his clutches.

By age nine many children have an almost obsessive interest in death and they may sound morbid at times. It is a very scary time for them because they are trying to develop a perspective on what death is all about. They talk to each other if adults won't listen and it really is important that they have their own questions answered, even if the answer is, "I don't know." If the questions are ignored, they soon learn to quit asking.

From Ten to Twelve

Children in this age group are ready to deal with the reality of death but they have learned something new which is very difficult for most of them to fully accept. *Death can happen to anybody at any age*. No one is immune for any period of time at all. There was comfort earlier in accepting human death as a phenomenon of aging and therefore there was no need to worry about it or even think about it happening *to them* for a long time. By the time children are ten they know that that is not true, and they must struggle with developing a philosophy which accepts but still defends them against daily vulnerability. Most children in this age group have outgrown their belief in their magical powers to bring death to a person by wishing it or saying it, but they need to be reassured that they have not caused deaths to happen in their families or to their friends by things they actually did or did not do. Many children feel responsible for such deaths, but too often they can't talk about it, they can't share their fears in order to gain absolution. I think teachers should be very alert to this possibility.

Age ten to twelve is a very anxious period for facing the reality of death, but many children deal with their anxiety by developing an elaborate facade. They joke about and make fun of death, and create fantastic stories about skeletons and ghosts which they swear are true. It is a period of great one-upmanship, and they may laugh uproariously as though the whole subject is very funny. Most of them really don't think it is so funny, they are just trying to protect themselves from a very fearful and a very dangerous unknown.

Adolescence

The practice of making fun of and joking about death continues into adolescence, but something new has been added and that is a defiance, a kind of "I dare it to happen to me" stance. Many of them have a tremendous need to prove over and over again that they are immune. For example in *Morante's Autobiography of an Italian Boy*, Arturo says:

> The thing I most hated was death. In my own natural happiness I chased all my thoughts away from death. But at the same time the more I hated death, the more I exaltedly enjoyed giving proofs of my own temerity. No game was enough fun if it lacked the element of risk.[6]

The risk taking behavior of many adolescents, their games of Chicken and Russian Roulette, their driving, drug use, hitchhiking may very well be related to their natural developmental stage of defiance about danger and death.

SERIOUSLY ILL AND BEREAVED CHILDREN IN THE SCHOOL SETTING

In the May 1974 issue of *The Journal of School Health*, the article "School Management of the Seriously Ill Child," by Kaplan, Smith and Grobstein said:

> The seriously ill child of school age poses difficult management problems for school administrators and teachers who are responsible for the education and health of their children. School teachers and administrators can meet the needs of all their children more effectively if they become aware of their own reactions to serious illness and understand how these personal responses may prejudice the judgments and decisions they must make on behalf of the seriously ill child. The child's ability to cope with a serious illness is largely dependent on the behavior of adults in his immediate environment.[7]

For purposes of this paper, seriously ill children refers primarily to those children who have incurable diseases, many of whom will presently die. These children are extremely vulnerable children but their classmates are too, to a lesser degree. The classroom teachers are perhaps most directly and most intimately involved with these hurting children, but the whole school team needs to be involved to some degree, especially in the support system that surrounds a particular teacher when he or she is coping with an extremely difficult problem. The school nurse should also be very intimately involved with these terminally ill children and their families; and also with the teachers.

What I have to say about this subject are "suggestions only" for school personnel to ponder. It would be presumptuous for me to try to tell teachers and others "what to do" and I won't.

Not many children die, of course, but a few do. Not many children are bereaved, either, but a few are. Approximately one child in twenty loses mother, father, or sibling by death before he reaches his 20th birthday, and considerably more than that experience the deaths of other significant relatives and friends. In addition, in the school setting, we have to consider definitely the bereavement aspects of husband and wife separation by divorce, long term illness, imprisonment or military service. (To some extent, the school-age children who are being reared by their single, never married mothers may be experiencing a different type of bereavement which could have important educational implications.)

The Seriously Ill [or Dying] Child

This is the child who is in or out of school, most likely in modern times in *and* out of school, because of new drugs and treatments which lead to more frequent and longer remissions. The child might have a severe heart problem, cystic fibrosis, other congenital or acquired disease, leukemia or other cancer. Many times this child has a grossly altered physical appearance; many times his emotional balance is precarious.

Anyone working with this child should be as natural as possible, open, honest, receptive, sincere, perceptive, caring. I emphasize the caring. (Of course this is how we should be with all children—with all people—but it is particularly important that the incurably ill child receive acceptance, approval and affection.) A facade of forced cheerfulness is to be avoided—not natural cheerfulness—that's great—but the overdone variety. All children respond negatively to phoniness. Also to be avoided, of course, is an attitude of doom and gloom.

It is important to ask the child periodically how things are going, and to listen to what he tells you. Ask if and how you can help, and follow through on what you are told. Of course, the teacher, the social worker, the nurse, the principal or anyone else in the school system is *not* the person to tell the child he is dying *if he is*. This is the parents' right, responsibility and privilege.

But if you listen, the *child may tell you;* and may very much need to tell someone. Often these seriously ill children cannot talk to their parents about what they fear, about what they think is happening, and not to their doctors on an out-patient basis because their parents are with them. It is not that parents do not want to help their suffering children—of course they do, but they are so emotionally involved and the children feel this acutely.

Most of the time the school person does not have to say very much at all. The important thing is to listen and then check out *with the child* what the two of you might do about whatever it is the child told you or asked you. You should make a plan of action together, and then help him to carry it out.

I have a very strong conviction that school personnel should keep in touch with the family of the dying child even though there is other educational input, like from homebound or hospital sources, or even when the child no longer has any educational input at all because he has become too sick. The child and his parents need to know, to be told over and over again, that the child is not forgotten, that he is remembered and cared about. It might make dying easier, whatever his age. Beautiful opportunities for education about death exist for the classmates of these dying children, when the teachers and nurses and others can skillfully and sensitively utilize them.

Some kind of follow-up with the family after the death is also highly desirable. Very often this might be by the school nurse. The family may not want continued contact, or contact at all, but most people respond positively to a sincere, "How are you doing?" inquiry. If they reject the contact, of course their wishes are respected.

The Death of an Elementary School Child

The death might be sudden, by accident or acute illness, or from prolonged illness. The circumstances influence how the subject is approached, but in my opinion the death must *never never* be ignored. I think that the children should be gathered together by their teacher and the death explained in simple, open, honest terms, in keeping with how old they are. The teacher might want to team up with a social worker, nurse, counselor, psychologist, even a knowledgeable funeral director, to do this.

The children need to know the cause of the death in order for them to make some assessment about how vulnerable they themselves are. "Am I next?" is a very real fear in childhood, especially in early childhood when most of them believe that children don't die. They need the opportunity to ask questions and to get straight answers. We don't have to know all the answers, of course. Ignoring the questions or hedging on them is what I think is wrong. I feel that parents in that child's room need to be told that a death occurred. Perhaps with the present privacy laws you may not be able to refer to the child by name—your school administration could give guidance on that. But parents do have the right to know that their child was exposed to a death. Children do not always tell everything they know at home, and the parents may not know. These other children may be exhibiting some hard-to-understand behavior which could be understood, if the parents knew what had happened. It is important to watch the children for some of the stages in the mourning process, particularly anger, guilt, depression. Particular children may need to talk individually about their feelings because so many times they feel responsible in one way or another, which adults might not even think about.

I think it is very important that professionals *not* impose their own religious beliefs on roomsful of chil-

dren, no matter how well intentioned they might be. (An exception would be in a parochial school.) Why do I say this? Well, for one reason, the separation of church and state, but it is more than that. There are too many variations in religious viewpoints and one could cause deeper confusion and deeper fear in the children than they are already experiencing. Catholic, Protestant, Unitarian, Jewish, Eastern, agnostic, atheistic viewpoints are all different and they all exist in our communities. Each person thinks his or her own viewpoint is right and usually would not want young children exposed to drastically different viewpoints, particularly as expressed by the teacher. Certainly we can allow the children to exchange their own religious ideas if they want to, emphasizing that different people believe different things.

Death of a Junior High or High School Student

Most of these are sudden, by accident or suicide, but a few are from long-term diseases. Again, the death should not be ignored. The homeroom teacher and other teachers should mention to the classes that the death happened. It is appropriate to say "I am having a bad time about it," if that is true. The opportunity should be given to the class to ask questions or to talk about it if they want to. If they don't want to, that's O.K. By bringing it up for discussion the students get the message that they may discuss the matter privately with that teacher if they need or want to. If they want to talk as a group it can be a very relevant and meaningful, perhaps even therapeutic, experience. The primary business of that class for that day could very well be death rather than English or math or science or whatever.

The Bereaved Child

Again the teacher is most directly involved with school children, but support and assistance from other school personnel is usually welcomed. When the death has been a parent or a sibling, that child's life is definitely changed and expectations will have to be modified while he or she is coping with the crisis. Children react to a family death in different ways. Some of them become withdrawn and sad and some of them become very boisterous and noisy so that people may think they don't even care. Usually they care very much but they may not know how to handle the enormity of their feelings. Some children may not show very much reaction at all.

The bereaved child should be given the opportunity to talk if he wants to, but should not be forced to. Some children are very private people, just as some adults are, whereas other children are very verbal and even enjoy the limelight aspects. Even if the child does not mention the death, the teacher should tell him *privately* that he or she heard about it, that it may be very hard for awhile, that if he wants to talk about it, someone is there—the teacher, the nurse, the counselor, the social worker. Many team members can carry this function if they are willing to.

The bereaved child often feels very isolated and alone; and he actually is. Other children don't know how to handle it either, and so they tend to avoid him. The child needs to feel cared about and supported and accepted as he gradually gets reintegrated into the group.

Death of Grandparent, Other Relatives, Friends

These can all be very significant deaths for children but the impact varies according to the closeness of the relationship. For example, the death of a grandmother living in the home is very different than the death of a grandmother who lives in another country and whom the child has never seen. These deaths all need to be acknowledged and we need to listen carefully if the child shares this information. If we have heard about it and the child has not mentioned it, it is important for us to mention it to him, again giving him permission to talk about it or not, as he wishes. Sometimes we won't even know, and the child will be struggling with a crisis all by himself.

Death of a Pet

Very often the first meaningful experience a child has with death is when a pet dies. This can be a very significant, very painful experience and should be handled with sensitivity and concern.

DEATH EDUCATION IN THE SCHOOLS

Education is supposed to prepare young people for life, and certainly death is a dimension of life. Of course, this education also belongs in the home and in the church, but it often is an avoided issue in the home, and many children do not go to church. Conversely, they almost all go to school, and schools have faculties who are knowledgeable in education process and in curriculum development and who have the skills necessary to get themselves ready to teach this important subject. Getting ready is a tremendously important aspect and it means a great deal of reading, talking, self-study, and thinking on the subject, so that the teacher can face up to his or her own death and to the deaths of loved ones.

Our young children are growing up in a society that tries to avoid aging and death. I definitely think that it is easier for children to handle death when it happens in their families if they have a kind of educational conditioning beforehand, if they learn to talk about death, if they learn to use the language of death, and if they learn to accept the fact that death really does happen to everyone. They will not have to use up so much energy in fear and in avoidance during a death crisis if the subject has become somewhat familiar to them.

I feel very strongly that children have to learn about this part of life before they come face-to-face with a devastating separation experience, and that preparing them is the job of the responsible adults in their lives, particularly their parents but also their clergy and their teachers.

All of us have responsibility for helping children learn about the phenomenon of death, to help them understand and accept that death is an integral part of the life cycle. Death is absolutely as real a part of life as birth is. One point marks the beginning; the other its ending. In the final analysis, death occurs exactly as often as birth—every person who is born must also die. It is as simple as that.

References

1. *Symp* 11, Group for the Advancement of Psychiatry, Death and Dying. New York, Mental Health Materials Center, Inc., 1965, p. 661.

2. Plant JS: *The Envelope*. New York, The Commonwealth Fund, 1950, p. 41.

3. Page H: *Playtime in the First Five Years*. New York, JB Lippincott, 1954, p. 125.

4. Feifel H (ed): *The Meaning of Death*. New York, McGraw-Hill Book Co., 1959, pp. 22–23.

5. Ilg FD, Ames L: *Child Behavior*. New York, Harper and Bros, 1955, pp. 311–13.

6. Talbot T (ed): *The World of the Child*. Garden City, NY, Doubleday and Co., Inc., 1967, p. 336.

7. Kaplan D, Smith A, Grobstein R: School management of the seriously ill child. *J School Health* 44:250, 1974.

Effects of Experiences with Loss and Death Among Preschool Children

by Estelle Parness

Human experiences of, and responses to, loss—primarily loss through death—have received increasingly widespread attention. Social, cultural and personal attitudes toward death and dying are being explored in psychological and medical literature. Styles of grieving and mourning in response to death are being identified and examined for their potentially pathogenic or healing features. More recently, the relationship between children's early experiences of loss and the course of their development has also been studied.

Loss And Death As Developmental Events

Grief and mourning, terms long reserved to describe adult reactions to the death of a loved or significant figure, can now be considered appropriate descriptions of responses by infants, toddlers and preschool children, for young children also experience loss and grief and display mourning. Most significant within the wide range of such experiences is the loss of a mother through separation or death. Failure to thrive, prolonged and delayed recuperation from infection, illness and hospitalization have been identified as some of the most apparent *physical* results of deprivation caused by a child's prolonged separation from his or her mother.

John Bowlby's contributions in recognizing and understanding the young child's grieving response to disruption of the mother-infant tie have, perhaps more than any other works, compelled us to consider the *manner* in which the infant, toddler and preschool child experience and express loss and grief.[1] Bowlby's works deal primarily with the instinctive basis for human attachment and with the disruptive effects of ill-timed, prolonged and intrusive separations on the developing child. It has become clear through his works that, beginning at approximately six to seven months, the infant experiences and mourns a particular kind of loss: separation from mother. Disruptive separations, both brief and extended, may be the earliest experiences of loss in a child's life, setting precedents for the content of his or her later responses to separation, loss and even death. Later childhood and adult reactions to losses of many kinds may be deeply influenced by the timing, frequency, and conditions of early separation and reunions.

Loss In Early Childhood

The child under the age of five has many encounters with separation, loss and death. Only recently have we become aware of the numbers and significance of these experiences. Our past inattention to the "small" losses of children has been a function, perhaps, of adults' self-protective attitudes. For to be aware of and responsive to a child's manner of expressing grief over the loss of a pet or other love object, one must often relive his own losses during childhood or later years. Gilbert Kliman of the Center for Preventive Psychiatry describes a 2-week survey in the Center's nursery school.[2]

"There were only 16 children in this group, but within a 2-week period the following events were recorded in the children's lives: a tonsillectomy, the injury of a relative in a car crash, sudden hospitalization of a sister in the middle of the night, a brother's operation, the death of a grandmother, a prolonged parental absence due to a 2-month trip abroad, the death of a turtle, the death of a cat, and revelation to a child's family that an uncle had died during the preceding months. Several weeks later, an aunt died and a child's cousin had a hernia operation (both in the same family). Considering that only 16 children were involved in this informal study, and that some events probably escaped the researcher's notice, there appears a rather high incidence level of life's crises. Yet it is probably not an unusual series. It is, after all, impressive to think of the number of aunts, uncles, cousins, grandparents, neighbors, friends, siblings and classmates in one child's life."

It is likely that any nursery school, Head Start program, child care center or family with young children would find comparable incidents in an informal survey of the experiences of the children in their care. For professionals whose work brings them into daily contact with children under the age of five, loss and death have now become critical issues for exploration, since the ability to recognize and respond to the child's way of expressing grief and mourning may deeply influence his successful mastery of life's developmental tasks.

Let us first elaborate on what may be typical experiences for many young children.

• A pet mouse dies in the Head Start classroom. The children insist on a funeral, burying the mouse in a shallow grave. When they ask why the mouse died, the teacher replies that he was sick. The next day, one of the children, John, is home with a cold. His closest friend in school, Carl, repeatedly asks why John is "gone" and has difficulty accepting the teacher's factual explanation. At "outside" time a group of children, including Carl, return to the dirt plot and proceed to dig up the dead mouse. They seem relieved to discover it is still there. After poking and prodding the mouse, all but Carl leave. Squatting, Carl peers intently at the exposed mouse and he is quiet and withdrawn for the rest of the morning. When his mother picks him up at the end of the day, he seems particularly clingy and anxious to leave.

• Danny, age 2½, is told that his grandfather has entered the hospital. When Grandfather does not return, Danny's parents tell him simply that he died and went to heaven. They try very hard not to cry in front of Danny. A year later Danny's mother is pregnant with her second child. As the time of delivery approaches, Danny refuses to go to nursery school, follows his mother closely about, and makes nightly excursions into his parents' bedroom. The day his mother goes to the hospital he is hysterical and inconsolable.

• Four-year old Debby's younger sister must go weekly to a large medical center for treatment of a malignant eye condition. Debby accompanies her mother and sister on these mornings. Later, in her nursery school, Debby becomes alternately withdrawn and unaccountably aggressive towards her friends. Concerned, the teacher senses a connection with the younger child's illness, but hesitates to talk with the mother, since implied is the possibility of the sister's death.

What do these events mean to the children? Are the subjects of death and the feelings surrounding the event appropriate ones for exploration in the preschool setting? How can and should teachers respond?

Studying Children's Ideas About Death

Within the past decade, research probing children's understanding of and response to death has slowly begun to emerge. These studies come from two main sources: the hospitalized and sometimes dying child and the healthy child in his natural environment. Some investigators have emphasized the limits of the child's understanding of the irreversibility of death as a function of his intellectual stage of development.[3] Studies with dying children have in the main been conducted with verbal, school-age children. This research has consistently revealed themes of intense loneliness, anxiety and isolation in the children' responses, as well as far greater awareness than anticipated on the part of the children of the terminal nature of their illnesses. Healthy children within the same age group seem to be limited in their understanding of death as final: comprehension seems to begin at about the age of seven or eight.

Easson, in his work *The Dying Child,* concludes that the dying preschool child, egocentric in his thinking and limited in his ability to formulate abstractions such as causality, time and finality, is incapable of perceiving death as permanent.[4] How then are we to explain the sometimes intense reactions of children under the age of five to separation, death and loss or, equally puzzling, their seeming absence of feeling? Are the children who display intense reactions in the examples given above behaving pathologically? Are children who seem to accept death matter-of-factly being "protected" by the limits of their chronological age and intellectual development?

While research on preschoolers' cognitive development would lead us to believe that they cannot conceive of the finality of death, anecdotal accounts of the young child's responses to separation, loss and death compel us to widen our exploration beyond the limits of a child's cognitive development. Anecdotal accounts provide us with access to

another dimension of the experience of loss and death in the preschool child: his inner emotional life as revealed through his behavior and, particularly, his play and drawings.

A separated toddler may grieve and mourn, display searching and longing with all the intensity of an adult mourning the death of a loved figure. Paradoxically, an older preschool child may appear to accept the news of the death of a parent impassively. The same toddler may greet the mother who is returning from a temporary separation with indifference and/or anger, while the preschooler may insist that the dead parent will be present for his next birthday.

While it is important to be aware of the unique manner in which young children perceive the world, some events may have greater power in the life of a child than others because of their significance for the child's survival. Thus, Bowlby has taken the issue of separation one critical step further: as the disruption of an instinctive tie that a young child may perceive as threatening his very survival. Bowlby's works strongly suggest that child and adult patterns of mourning are fundamentally the same and represent an instinctive human need to be in contact with another whose presence may be experienced as, or actually represent, survival. Such a view of separation, loss and death and the responses to them places these experiences within a developmental framework, rather than outside ordinary human experience—as deviant or pathological.

To move towards another, particularly in times of stress, to display intense anger, protest, yearning and searching at separation or in response to loss through death are characteristic responses displayed by children and adults throughout the human lifespan. The developmental course of such patterns are naturally influenced by a child's cognitive development. Unless, however, we recognize the instinctive basis for the need for relatedness we may be mystified by the intensity and paradoxical nature of responses to ruptures in relations. Such behavior becomes more comprehensible as an expression of the human organism's adaptive efforts toward survival and broadens the range of normalcy in responses accompanying these events.

Helping Young Children

Adults who are important in children's lives can help them only if they are prepared to explore their own attitudes and anxieties about separation, loss and death. To the extent that we are able to confront and explore our own perceptions and feelings on this issue (just as with sexuality, aggression and tenderness), to that extent will we function more appropriately with children. This suggests the need for opportunities for teachers, doctors and nurses, as well as parents, to engage in such exploration. The loneliness and isolation of dying children referred to previously was particularly pronounced in settings where adult helpers engaged in denial both of their own feelings of helplessness, anger and sadness and of the signals and cues coming from young patients expressing the same feelings.

Coinciding with such self-exploration are opportunities for preschool teachers to exploit the unique sensitivity they often display with the non-verbal cues children give, primarily through play. Play has long been recognized as an avenue to the child's perceptions, feelings and ideas about his world. The significance of play, through its function of enabling the young child to gain information about his world, assumes new proportions when viewed in the context of the child's response to loss and death. An alert, sensitive teacher will be able to see how a child's seemingly paradoxical and/or indifferent responses to such events are disguises to be shed in the comfort, familiarity and spontaneity of a play setting.

In exploring feelings with young children, we must allow ourselves to take cues from the child, since avoidance of, as well as approach to, play materials tells much about the child's concerns. Self-initiated play permits the child to develop his own theme and to describe his understanding of the loss. It also allows him to set the limits he needs at that time. Encouraging such exploratory play implies an acceptance of the child's strong feelings, despite his cognitive limitations and *apparent* distortions of reality.

Carl's concern over his friend's absence from school, the day after the pet mouse was buried, for example, also reflected experiences within his family around the death of an infant cousin. Adults (perhaps in an effort to protect him *and* themselves) had ceased talking about the infant's death whenever Carl entered the room, and they had excluded the youngest children from the funeral. The cues in Carl's behavior at school, then, while not forming a complete nor coherent picture of his inner concerns, were signals of connections he was making between sickness (a cold) and death. If unexplored, such connections can contribute threateningly to a child's sense of personal vulnerability, as well as to that of significant attachment figures such as mothers, fathers and teachers. Several avenues are open for an adult to assist a child but none is more important than making oneself available to help him explore his feelings.

Teachers can alert mothers, encouraging them to share ongoing experiences in the home around such events as divorce, separation, illness, hospitalization and death, as well as injuries to pets and scenes on television, for all are relevant to the formation of the child's view of loss and of the acceptability and expression of his own feelings. Testimony as to the peculiar and intense impact of such early experiences on later life is becoming increasingly available, not the least of which is our reluctance as adults to explore this area, both within ourselves and with the child.

As a teacher finds the topic of loss and accompanying feelings more acceptable through self-exploration, children's preoccupation with and struggles around their related experiences become more apparent and their expression is encouraged. Both child and adult are then freer to use spontaneous events in the classroom to explore feelings, thoughts and ideas about change, growth, separations and death.

The child who became fearful that his mother might die (disappear and never return) when she went to the hospital, as his hospitalized grandfather did, may suddenly cling to his mother at times of separation, or he may show angry rejection or avoidance of his mother at reunion. Fear regarding his own bodily integrity may be expressed in an acute reaction to a minor injury while playing, or in preoccupation with such broken toys as a doll with a missing arm or leg. "Being dead" to the young child may mean having dirt in the face, being buried "alive" or being suffocated, as well as the fact of never seeing loved ones again. As a result, a child may suddenly exhibit night fears and refuse to go to bed. Such behavior, when viewed within the context of the power of the experience of separation, loss and death, and threatening to relationships

that are necessary to survival, clearly has developmental origins, patterns and a natural history well within the range of normal human experience and response. Information or simple reassurances which are designed to "correct" a distorted perception may remain unprocessed if the child's behavior is viewed as deviant and underlying feelings are ignored.

Sudden, sometimes violent, loss such as occurs with suicide or accidental death is a crisis for all: the child, his family, friends and teacher. Acknowledgement of feelings by adults significant to the child is appropriate and often the clearest response possible amidst the inevitable confusion that follows. Avoidance or denial of sadness and/or anger may become a source of distortion and mystification, entangling the child in the struggle of adults around him in their efforts to sort out their own feelings of responsibility. Anger and protest, however "irrational" they may appear to be upon the death of or separation from an attachment figure, have been clearly identified by Bowlby and others as normal adaptive responses.

The serious illness of the sibling of a young child is now known to have important emotional consequences for that child as well. Debby, the child whose younger sister was seriously ill, revealed through her drawings and play the theme of a little girl who: "was in jail and had no way to get out. Someone had locked her up . . . she didn't know who and she couldn't get out . . . she was crying . . . she had broken someone's arm."

Overcome with guilt about her sister's illness, aware of her parents' anxiety as expressed in the special attention given her sister at home, Debby was frightened by her own feelings. Debby's teacher, who struggled to overcome her own resistance to an awareness of the issue of death, was better able to gain an understanding of Debby's behavior and subsequently to offer her many opportunities to explore her feelings and to talk more openly about her sister's illness. Guilt-provoking connections Debby had earlier made between fights with her sister, punches to the eye, and the sister's illness—connections revealed in her drawings—were gradually clarified.

The child under the age of five is forming fundamental ideas and feelings about the world he lives in. Initially this world centers around his family, primarily his mother and father. As he grows, his world expands to include events, individuals and institutions outside the family. With the advent of television, Head Start, day care centers and nursery schools, these external forces impinge on the young child's consciousness much earlier than in previous years. Among these early experiences are the child's contact with the medical world. While much attention, thought and literature have been devoted to the school's influence as an institution, relatively little attention has been paid to the later effects of early medical experiences. For most children, these experiences begin in early infancy, are frequent in the preschool years and include acquaintance with doctors, nurses and the hospital.

The Hospital As A Symbol

As perceived by the young child—whether through direct personal experience, through that of a member of his family, as a visual experience or through hearsay—the hospital may affect the child's growing inner "set" toward human loss and death. How can we assist the child under five who must himself enter the hospital?

The symbol of the hospital as a place where people experience pain, separation from important and loved figures and, frequently, death is slow to change. Television programs, conversations overheard by children and the reality of hospital practices themselves have contributed to the creation of this symbol. Central to the outcome of a young child's hospitalization experience is the extent to which his mother is allowed to accompany him, participate in his care, and to be continuously present.

If hospital practices do not permit the continued presence of the mother, or if the mother cannot be available for the child's hospitalization, preparation becomes *preparation for separation* first. Substitution of other family members or well-trained surrogate mothers (play therapists) is a second aspect of preparation, and finally there is preparation for the medical event itself. Crucial to the child's impending hospitalization is the family's advance knowledge of the particular hospital's policy regarding the continued presence of the mother. Research evidence is growing that *no loss to a little child is greater,* particularly when under stress, than that of the mother's sudden and unexpected disappearance.

Today, research to clarify additional methods of preparing children for medical events, before or during the hospitalization itself, suggests major changes in hospital practices that deeply affect children.[5]

The nursery school, Head Start classroom or child care center, where the young child spends much time and forms many close attachments, can play an important role in assisting with this preparation.

The age of the child, the degree of stress anticipated, inclusion of the parents in the preparation experience whenever possible, timing the preparation so that it is neither too far in advance (which increases the child's anxiety) nor too close to the event (which offers insufficient time for the child to ponder, question and prepare himself internally) are all important considerations. Teachers need to be aware of the importance of having available in the classroom such special play materials as stethoscopes, play syringes, mirrors, dolls, cotton, white coats, bandaids, etc. These are easily obtained and should be ready for the child before and after the hospital experience. Post-hospitalization play in a protected setting with teacher and friends frequently involves reliving the experience and clarifying perceptions and feelings.

Response To Loss: Regressive Or Adaptive?

Very young children have resiliency and fortitude in the face of some of the painful and unpredictable experiences life has to offer. Nevertheless, adults still strive to identify and modify those experiences of life that create unnecessary and critical vulnerability for the child's later productive adult functioning. We should also concern ourselves with the immediate impact on the child.

In evaluating our approach, we may see that we have, perhaps, allowed ourselves to focus too intently on the "pathological symptom." A child who insists on being close to mother after a period of separation, who may behave in ways we have come to regard as regressive (clinging, thumb-sucking, lap-sitting, temporary bed wetting, demanding a bottle after weaning) may, in fact, be engaging in behavior that is adaptive. For all such behavior engages the most important attachment figure—mother—in close caretaking, reminiscent to the child of the complete safety of an earlier pre-separation

period. When seen this way, as re-establishing a continuity of safety and caretaking that has been interrupted, the child's behavior is far more understandable.

In gauging our effectiveness in helping young children with experiences of loss and death we must, of course, be aware that our ultimate impact may not be apparent until years later. Nevertheless, there are important ongoing signs we can be alert to. For example, does the child move towards, or away from, life? (Excessive, unrelenting preoccupation with death can be an avoidance of living.)Is the child able, after an experience of loss, to return in a reasonable time to play that is predictive of his continued forward movement and growth?

The young child who seems immobilized by anxiety and unable to rejoin age-appropriate activities, playmates and settings over an extended period of time may need special help. However, even when confronted with such behavior, we must look for the reality-based elements that are usually part of the child's experiences. Thus, what we have long regarded as school phobias (intrinsically irrational if regarded as phobias) have been described by Bowlby as representing genuine and realistic fears of loss of an attachment figure in the home due to parents' fighting or the threat of divorce or emotional withdrawal.

If we can remember that what we have become accustomed to thinking of as "regressive" tendencies are really not chronic or pathological but frequently temporary and adaptive reactions of the child, and that such loss and mourning go on all through life, it becomes easier to allow the child and ourselves such means of responding.

Although one cannot prepare children for the unpredictable events of life, sudden accidental deaths and loss must be dealt with. Here, the opportunities for after-work are always available. We can engage in work with young children that begins with the assumption of loss as a universal human experience. We can also keep in mind children's abilities to experience and respond to our efforts to assist them in integrating such loss. Through our honesty and willingness to explore our feelings and share children's experiences of grief, we speak to them of confidence in their resources, resiliency and power over their future lives—in spite of the unexpected.

Much remains to be understood about the earliest experiences of loss and their later effects. Nursery school teachers and others who spend much time with the young child under five and are professionally known for their sensitive observations should extend that sensitivity to an important part of the life of the child—loss and death.   ■

---

[1] Bowlby, J., "Grief and Mourning in Infancy," *Psychoanalytic Study of the Child,* International Universities Press, New York, 1960; Bowlby, J., *Attachment and Loss, Vol. I. Attachment,* Basic Books, New York, 1969 and *Attachment and Loss, Vol. II. Separation,* Basic Books, New York, 1973.

[2] Kliman, G. K., *Psychological Emergencies of Childhood,* Grune and Stratton, New York, 1968.

[3] See Koocher, Gerald P., "Why Isn't the Gerbil Moving Anymore?", CHILDREN TODAY, Jan.-Feb. 1975.

[4] Easson, W., *The Dying Child,* Charles C Thomas, Springfield, Illinois, 1970.

[5] See Azarnoff, P. and Flegal, S., *A Pediatric Play Program,* Charles C Thomas, Springfield, Illinois, 1975; Azarnoff, P., "Mediating the Trauma of Serious Illness and Hospitalization in Childhood," CHILDREN TODAY, July-August 1974; and Johnson, Beverley H., "Before Hospitalization: A Preparation Program," CHILDREN TODAY, Nov.-Dec. 1974.

Reactions of Pupils and Teachers to Death in the Classroom

Charles R. Keith
David Ellis

The burgeoning of literature in the past 20 years on death and its personal impact indicates that the subject of death, like sex, is emerging from tabooed status. Our cultural practices, concerning death and dying have been held up for critical re-examination (Mitford 1962).

In the medical field, procedures surrounding dying and how to die with dignity have been openly examined in the lay press, medical literature, and important court decisions. In fields specifically dealing with dying children, such as pediatrics, the commonly held assumptions that preadolescent children are incapable of conceptualizing death have given way under the impact of many studies showing that children think about, react to, and are quite troubled about dying.

Articulate students of the subject, such as Kübler-Ross (1969), actively advocate training of those who care for the dying to address the subject and to assist the child and his family to master and come to terms with the reality of death. Furman (1974) presents striking evidence that three- and four-year-old children are able to conceptualize the permanence of death, and to master loss through a mourning process. She emphasizes that young children can do this if they have attained adequate personality development appropriate for their chronological age and only if they have the intuitive, verbalized support of their caretaking adults. Because the prerequisites are so often not present, it is not surprising to Furman that so many older children and even adults are unable to handle the death of an important person in their lives. Furman emphasizes that because some children at a particular age are unable to conceptualize death and to mourn is not the same as saying that all children of that age lack the development to do so. This variability in maturational levels of children helps account for several conflicting studies, some of which show elementary school age children as not concerned about death (Natterson & Knudson 1960), whereas others reveal the same age children are quite concerned and anxious about death (Meleor 1973). Variability also springs from the differing methods used to elicit children's fantasies and ideas about death. For instance, children in intensive therapy (Furman 1974), would be expected to reveal anxiety-laden fears and magical ideas about death due to the support of the therapeutic relationship whereas studies using single interviews and direct questioning techniques would be expected to elicit much more denial concerning death anxiety.

Child psychoanalysts have known for a long time that children interpret death in terms of crucial developmental fears at particular ages. Death for the preschooler is often equated with separation and abandonment and viewed as a punishment for hostile wishes toward the deceased. In the older child who has formed a conscience, there is the addition of guilt for death wishes, and the child may feel responsible for another's death. These childhood anxieties, springing primarily out of the normal magical thinking of the young child, make it much more difficult for adults to talk about death directly with children, since adults carry remnants of these childhood fears within themselves. In addition, the topic may arouse defensiveness and anxiety in the child.

Considering the reactions to death of a pupil in the classroom, it is not surprising from the foregoing discussion that little has been written about it in the educational, medical, or psychiatric literature. Wolfenstein and Kliman (1965) drew together observations from many settings describing children's reactions to the death of President Kennedy. McDonald (1963, 1964) vividly describes the reactions of a group of four- and five-year-old children in a therapeutic nursery to the death of a mother of one of their classmates. Harrison (1967) describes how the adult caretakers in a children's psychiatric inpatient unit found it difficult at times to help their child patients verbalize and master their concerns about President Kennedy's assassination due to their own adult anxieties and misperceptions. These studies arise from the sensitive observations of trained personnel conducting therapeutic groups for children where the emphasis is on verbalization and mastery of fears.

The question might be raised whether the focus on mastery of anxiety concerning death is appropriate for the normal classroom setting in the public school. The same objections raised about sex education could be raised about death education in the classroom; namely, that it is a personal, idiosyncratic, and anxiety-arousing topic that should be left for parents, religious educators, and therapeutic personnel to address rather than schools.

Whatever one's views on the appropriateness of discussing death in the classroom, occasional tragedies occur that force the issue; namely, the death of a pupil or teacher who has been a meaningful part of the classroom group. This came to the attention of the authors during the course of group consultation meetings with elementary school counselors. These counselors have met for several years in the Durham Community Guidance Clinic with the clinic staff and hence have formed an open, communicative relationship with the consultants.

Two years before the writing of this paper, several counselors mentioned the subject of death during the course of the consultation meetings and asked for a developmental scheme concerning how children view death at various age levels. As we discussed this topic, one of the counselors suddenly left the meeting room in tears. Upon returning, she said that the discussion reminded her of personal childhood experiences with death. At about the same time, a child at another counselor's school was accidentally killed. With the idea arising out of the consultation discussions, the counselor returned to her school and helped the children and staff address the issue of the pupil's death, rather than ignoring it. Out of this initial work we studied five pupil's deaths and one teacher's death the following year.

FORMAT OF THE INVESTIGATION

The investigation was set up along the following format. Whenever a child (age 6 to 12) in an elementary school died, the authors were notified by the counselor of the school. At that time, one of the authors would visit the school and interview the teacher or counselor. Depending on how the death of the child was handled by the individual school, one or more students from the dead child's classroom were interviewed. An open-ended, clinical interview style was used. At a later point, the counselor wrote up a brief explanation and commentary on how the situation was handled in the classroom and the school. The project was begun in October 1975, and continued until June 1976. The total number of deaths investigated was six. The project was set up not only to study the reactions in the school to a child's death but also to generate possible ways of dealing with the phenomenon after it occurred.

The following is a brief description of each of the six subjects, and the classroom in which the impact of the death was felt. The first subject was Ted, a seven-year-old boy in the second grade. He was playing in an area that was off limits to children, and was killed immediately when he fell to the ground from a height. Ted's death had a major impact on the activities in his class and in the school. The second subject was Laura, an eight-year-old girl enrolled in the third grade. She was killed instantly in an automobile accident in which her father was the driver. Laura's death caused a major impact on the activities of her class and

school. The third subject, Brad, was an eight-year-old boy enrolled in the third grade, who died in an automobile collision. The impact of this child's death on the school was not as observable as others. He had just moved to the area and was not known by the other children. The fourth subject, Jamie, was a nine-year-old, fourth-grade boy. He was killed in a shooting accident. The boy who accidentally shot him lived in the same neighborhood, and knew many of the children in the school. The impact on other children was profound. The child's death appeared to cause disturbances in all areas of school activities, and particularly in the dead child's classroom. The fifth subject, Steve, was a third-grade, eight-year-old boy. He slowly died of leukemia. His disappearance from the school was a gradual one, with his materials and articles slowly being withdrawn from the classroom. The sixth subject was a second-grade teacher. The woman was 30 years of age, single, and a dedicated teacher. Her sudden death was caused by pneumonia complications. Her pupils had seen her feeling well on a Friday only to learn the following Monday that she had died during the weekend.

RESULTS

The results of the investigation showed two principal methods of coping by school personnel. The elementary school personnel appeared either to deal directly with the death of one of their students or to ignore it completely. During the interview sessions with different school professionals (i.e., counselors, teachers, or principals), the extent to which the professional felt comfortable with the death appeared to correlate with the administrative decisions concerning how the death of a school child would be handled.

The method of ignoring a child's death varied in form, but the general procedure was to avoid any mention of the death. The official reason given for ignoring the death was that discussion would keep the children stirred up. In the case of Jamie, where the child's death was ignored, officials abruptly removed the dead child's belongings, including the desk. The rest of the children's reaction to the event was fear. No questions were asked. A book, which had belonged to the dead child, was accidentally opened by one of

the children in the classroom. The child who opened the book saw the dead boy's name, screamed, and dropped the book. Even though most of the materials of the dead boy had magically disappeared during the night, the classmates carried his memory with them. The students spoke of Jamie's disappearance and the rumors of death they had heard. During snack breaks, recess, and other times, the children would gather and talk of the boy who had disappeared. The reactions of the adults appeared to communicate that Jamie's disappearance was a magical, terrible event, an event so horrible that no one could speak of it. The classroom effect consisted of restless behavior, an inability to concentrate, and a slight decrease in learning. The counselor requested a series of interviews with the teacher who gradually acknowledged that she was having trouble helping her class master the death of their classmate. She related her personal, painful experiences with death and how upset she had felt upon learning of the death of the child in her class. As they talked, she became more upset, because the death of this child apparently made her relive previous personal experiences she had faced with the loss of important persons in her life. This teacher's repression of her feelings had sufficed until she was faced with the death of her pupil.

When the approach was that of directly dealing with the death of a school child, there tended to be a general participation by all involved. The participation began with the principal, or at least his approval and included teachers, special personnel, and the dead child's classmates. The professionals met often as a group and planned a course of action. The principal, in one case, sent out a brief memo to all the school personnel informing them of the tragedy. Teachers were prepared for their classes to be upset and disruptive following the death. Each class was usually told of their classmate's death at the beginning of the day. Questions were encouraged and answered by the teacher. General discussions followed the death announcement, and the decision of what to do with the dead child's belongings was discussed by the class, as a prelude to making a group decision. The involvement of the children in the performing of active and mastery-oriented acts was considered important. The purchasing of flowers, signing a sympathy card, or planting a tree were all active symbolic gestures that were used to express grief. These were considered concrete actions in which the children could participate.

The following vignette describes further how school personnel actively grappled with a pupil's death.

In a group consultation meeting, a counselor was asked to review how she helped her school deal with a recent death of a pupil. She was emotionally involved, to the point of anguish, and her voice halted a number of times.

The counselor stated: "At the end of spring vacation a second grader, Ted, was killed. He fell while playing on a wire left hanging by the telephone company. He had attended the same school since the first grade and was well known and liked by his classmates.

When informed of her pupil's death, the concerned teacher came to me and asked: (a) how to handle the classroom and (b) what to expect in the next several days. Fortunately, she was a good teacher who had handled other stressful situations well when they arose in her classroom.

The class was told of Ted's death at the beginning of the day. Many of the children had already heard, as there had been newspaper coverage. The children were encouraged to ask questions but few were asked. Some questions asked were: "Is he dead?", "Where is he now?" and then the subject was spontaneously dropped though the teacher remained open for further comments.

Ted's name was erased from various lists in the room, such as room helper and rosters, as the pupils watched. His desk was emptied by the children, and everything of Ted's was removed from the classroom. Mothers of other children dropped by during the day and asked the teacher: "What should I do?"; "Should I take my children to the funeral?"

During the day, children surreptitiously asked to talk with the teacher. Some wanted to talk more about Ted's death, some did not mention it at all. Feeling as if something more should be done, the teacher and some of the parents decided to plant a tree in Ted's memory. A quiet and short ceremony was held during the school day during which a small tree was planted. The children were active in the planting and waterings. Some problems became evident during the weeks after Ted's death. The teacher had a big responsibility, for not only did she help the

children deal with the death of a classmate but she had to deal with it herself. She was much disturbed by the fact that the children so quickly "removed" him emotionally from the classroom on the day back from vacation that occurred shortly after the funeral. In addition, she was unofficial advisor to several parents about how to help their children deal with a situation which no one had had to deal with before. One of the most difficult aspects for the teacher was answering the question asked by the children: "Where is Ted?" The parents' home and religious instructions concerning death were unclear to the teacher, making her uncomfortable in giving specific answers. The parents of Ted asked to meet with the teacher to reminisce and obtain emotional support.

Difficulties cropped up during the rest of the year. The parents wanted to bring cupcakes and other refreshments on Ted's birthday. This was not allowed. Ted's mother asked to come and see the class several times and talk about Ted to them. This was not allowed either, since the pupils appeared to have mourned and were moving emotionally on to other issues as evidenced by a lighter emotional mood in the classroom, fewer questions and references concerning the deceased pupil, and an inner intuitive awareness within the teacher that she and her pupils had worked enough on the loss.

In the following school year, the original class composition did not change much. The class gradually settled back into usual routines, but the children from Ted's neighborhood who had seen his death had profound reactions. These children were worked with in various ways by the teacher.

Occasionally, the reaction of an emotionally disturbed child may be quite severe. After the death of a friend, one girl became distant, hard-to-reach, and extremely quiet. The child had an unstable family history and severe adjustment problems. The traumatic incident of the loss of a close friend appeared to tip the balance toward regression. She was referred for professional care. Children who are troubled with fantasies of annihilation, feelings of omnipotence, and high anxiety may be placed in a precarious emotional balance when an event appears to support their fantasies. These fragile children should be allowed to participate in the class activities arranged

to deal with the death of a classmate, but monitored closely. They may need special (i.e., counselor) attention.

CONCLUSION AND SUMMARY

Common sense along with many authorities, e.g., Clay (1976) and Kübler-Ross (1969), indicates that children should be prepared for death as they grow up. Therefore, the death of a classmate allows an excellent opportunity to explore with the dead child's friends and acquaintances what death means to them. Philosophical and religious questions may be asked. The fielding of these questions allows a broader grasp of what death represents. Exploring the cultural expectations (i.e., funeral, flowers, graveyard, tombstones, etc.) of death in the community allows a better understanding and grasp of the social realities of dying.

The results of this naturalistic study indicate that the feelings and reactions of pupils to a classmate's death may be facilitated or hindered by the behavior of the adults involved. The most powerful hindrance is the teacher's denial of the child's capacity to deal with death. The teacher who is open to the painful feelings aroused by death is also the best facilitator as he or she helps the class, as a unit, approach death as a phenomenon to explore together. The use of a counselor or outside agency may be needed for particular children, but the most effective method of handling children's reactions to the death of a classmate or teacher is within the classroom.

At first glance, it may appear that the classroom is troubled when pupils are curious and asking questions about a classmate's death, showing feelings, fears, or anxiety, and are unable to attend to learning tasks for a brief period. The impressions from this investigation, however, are that this classroom is the healthiest and the pupils have the best opportunity to master the trauma of a pupil's death and to then resume classroom learning in a relatively comfortable manner.

In those classrooms in which a pupil's death was not a subject of inquiry and in fact was suppressed, there appeared lingering tensions and a sense that an important subject is in the air but being avoided.

The following are recommendations that we have found helpful:

1.   Immediately upon news of a pupil's (or teacher's) death a meeting should be held including the involved teacher(s), principal, and school counselor to discuss the implications of the death, the relationship the pupil had with peers, and how the parents may participate in the subsequent classroom activities concerning the death.

2.   One or several of the above school personnel are then designated to discuss the death with the pupils, answer questions, and lead a class discussion. Hopefully, one of those will be the classroom teacher who has the ongoing relationship with the classroom. If she is too uncomfortable, then she can be present while someone else leads the discussion.

3.   Out of the discussion will evolve a plan of action for removal of the dead pupil's belongings, sending a group message of condolence to the family, and some type of memorial for the deceased pupil. Hopefully, the pupils will have a major input into the formulation of the plan, which should be simple and allow for closure within a reasonable time period. (e.g., planting a tree, which is a time-limited, well-defined activity).

4.   As these immediate postdeath activities end, the teacher will hopefully have administrative approval to be open to individual or group requests to discuss death either in terms of the deceased pupil or death in its more general aspects. This will not only provide a valuable learning experience as described in this paper but will also provide benchmarks for the teacher concerning the progress of her class in coming to terms with the death.

5.   The counselor and principal should continue to provide back-up for the teacher in terms of conversations or meetings to discuss how the class and the teacher are faring, to resolve issues of further family contacts regarding the death and possible ripple effects in other areas of school life.

REFERENCES

Clay, V. S. Children deal with death. *The School Counselor*, 1976, *25*, 175–183.

Furman, E. *A child's parent dies; Studies in childhood bereavement*. New Haven: Yale University Press, 1974.

Harrison, S. I. et al. Children's reactions to bereavement. Adult confusions and misperceptions. *Archives of General Psychiatry*, 1967, *17*, 593–597.

Kübler-Ross, E. *On death and dying*. New York: Macmillan, 1969.

McDonald, M. Helping children to understand death. *Journal of Nursery Education*, 1963, *19*, 19–25.

McDonald, M. Preschool reactions to death: Facts and feelings. *Psychoanalytic Study of the Child*, 1964, *19*, 358–376.

Meleor, J. Children's conceptions of death. *The Journal of Genetic Psychology*, 1973, *123*, 359–360.

Mitford, J. *The American way of death*. New York: Simon and Schuster, 1962.

Natterson, J., & Knudson, A. Observations concerning fear of death in fatally ill children and their mothers. *Psychosomatic Medicine*, 1960.

Wolfenstein, M., & Kliman, G. *Children and the death of a president*. New York: Doubleday, 1965.

Helping Children Accept Death and Dying through Group Counseling

by Constance D. Berg

This article suggests that the new wave of openness about death in our culture and the elimination of the death taboo will not be completely accomplished without developing a generalized practice in death counseling with children. A brief historical perspective of research confirms the necessity of including children in discussions about death education. A taped counseling session with several preadolescent boys in a rural midwestern school demonstrates the importance of accepting the deep feelings and fears that children must deal with in order to be free from unnatural anxiety about death and dying as adults.

The elimination of the death taboo may be hailed as one of contemporary society's great psychological accomplishments. Generalized practice in death counseling with children at all age levels must be accomplished, however, before eradication of the taboo can be truly claimed.

A taboo may be challenged successfully during the years without disturbing its inherent power to inhibit and repress natural curiosity and emotion. When potent emotions associated with taboos, such as fear and prejudice, are recognized and dealt with at early levels of individual consciousness, however, their influence can be overcome. The taboos of racism and sexism have been successfully challenged and dissipated to a degree, yet practical education for our children in these areas still creates powerful controversy and disputes in public forums.

Perhaps death education will not follow the same negative pattern, for we have undoubtedly experienced a phenomenal breakthrough without severe repercussions (Gordon & Klass 1977). The counseling profession in particular has dramatically changed its practices and attitudes toward death education during the past five years. The profession has gone from a position of ignoring death topics to complete recognition of the need for death counseling (Bascue & Krieger 1974; Berg 1973; Nelson & Peterson 1975; Reisler 1977). Educators in other disciplines have developed workshops, materials, and courses of study for all age levels (Mills, Reisler, Robinson & Vermilyne 1976; Stanford & Perry 1976). The Center for Death Education and Research and the Foundation of Thanatology have published comprehensive bibliographies dealing with the many aspects and problems of death in society (Fulton 1973; Kutscher & Kutscher 1974). Professionals are no longer free to hide behind a taboo.

The problem that we now face in an effort to eliminate death fears seems to be related to the fact that a taboo may be eliminated in adults and still exist in children. This is evidenced in an overview of the writing on the psychology of death. Beginning in the 1920s, few psychologists (including Freud) discussed children's attitudes on death. Schilder and Wechsler's study (1934) was the exception. Anthony (1940), Nagy (1948), Mahler (1950), and Bender (1953) wrote about children's responses to death long before the subject was of professional and popular interest. There were only a few researchers in our country, such as Alexander and Alderstein (1958) and Wolfenstein and Kliman (1965), who challenged the taboo in regard to children's attitudes about death. For the most part, children's responses were neglected and ignored.

At the adult level, Mitford (1963) and Kübler-Ross (1969) lifted the barrier and public discussion of death was no longer an indelicate matter; death became an acceptable topic of conversation. This phenomenal breakthrough occurred in education as well as in other disciplines.

Although I admit to a certain uneasiness in regard to the confidence with which we are forging ahead in death education, seeming to dismiss the insidious power of a long-standing taboo, I have been reassured by my experiences of counseling children in death education and believe that the death taboo may finally be broken.

Children will not risk ridicule nor rejection until they are assured that the significant adults in their lives will accept their questions and readiness to learn. This fact was impressed upon me two years ago when several preadolescent boys shyly asked me to meet with them to talk about death. Two older boys had encouraged them to suggest the possibility of forming a group to discuss death. They found that individual counseling following the death of the older boys' grandparents had been helpful.

Although all of the boys had known me throughout their primary years, it was interesting to find that not only sex but also death were subjects relegated to the privacy of locker rooms. Alexander and Alderstein's early claim that "during this period (latent) questions about death disappear from the conscious repertoire as though the matter is no longer of interest" (1958, p. 175) did not seem valid because these boys appeared anxious to ask me questions and discuss their fears. Perhaps this was due in part to the trust established between us during previous counseling sessions when we discussed their other concerns.

I was aware of the restrictions and restraints of the rural conservative community, which had rejected a proposal for sex education in its schools, so I requested that the boys obtain permission to participate in the group from their parents. After the parents indicated support and interest in the project, the boys and I planned to meet once a week for six weeks.

The major emphasis of the counseling sessions was to carefully deal with the strong but unexpressed emotions about death that were troubling the boys. The theory was that by discovering that their peers were also curious and fearful about death the boys would form a therapeutic bond that could alleviate their anxiety and help them gain a mature understanding of death.

As a counselor, I was prepared to lead discussions because I had studied and worked with individuals and families coping with death. This was to be a new approach for me, however, as none of the children had suffered a family loss, and I was uncertain how the sessions should be structured towards the trauma of death and dying. My tenuous security was based upon my faith that the children would guide me and find the answers they were seeking.

Throughout the discussions, I was impressed by the depth of feeling that the children released. These intense discussions can be transmitted more effectively through the children's own words. The following dialogue is from a discussion that occurred during the third meeting.

Counselor: I'd like to start today with this question; maybe we can go around the circle and whoever wants to can answer it. Think about it and see what you feel. Can you remember the first time you ever thought about death or dying, or began to wonder about it? Can you remember? You must have had some feelings when you first realized that things die. Was it a shock? Can you remember when you first realized that everything dies? Everything? Jim?

Jim: I think I was about 5—4 or 5—. *(Long silence)*

Counselor: Go ahead, Jim. And what did you wonder?

Jim: Well, I just thought, well, it was when, uh we'd had our cat for a long time, and it was the only cat I think we had ever had. We had two of them. One of them had kittens and stayed alive, but then one of them died. It just kind of worried me, you know, because I really didn't know what had happened to her, and I thought well it was just sleeping or something, and then it started to scare me, and I started to think—what happens after you get to be 200 years old?

Counselor: I see. You thought that maybe you would die, too, when you were around 200 years old and you didn't know what happened and felt scared.

I attempted to reflect on his unexpressed thought that death is inevitable. Any child of 4 thinks death is remote and not a universal eventuality, but now at 11 he was becoming ready to logically discuss the inevitability of his own death.

Jerry: Uh, when I was 8, I wasn't very old because I didn't know much about stuff like that. Well, I was watching TV, and these bullfighters were fighting, and he got gored and he died out there in the field and I didn't know what happened to him. I thought, He's trying to fake the bull out so he won't hurt him. And then they carried him off the field, and he was bloody and everything and then I got scared, real scared and I screamed, and I ran out the door and ran around about five times and came back into the house and shut off the TV and ran into my bed.

Counselor: You were really scared, Jerry. Were you all by yourself?

Jerry: No.

Counselor: Did your mother—?

Jerry: She didn't even know.

Counselor: She didn't know why you were crying?

Jerry: No I didn't scream until I got outside. She didn't hear me.

Counselor: So you didn't ask her anything about it at the time? *(Silence.)*

Children live in a world full of fear and threats. They tend to see violence everywhere and are ready to emulate this violence, although they hide their feelings from adults. Later in the discussion we learned that Jerry's attitudes about death were related to his own aggressiveness and fear of the sadistic character of death. He does not fear dying as much as he fears being murdered. Bender's (1953) studies confirm this observation in regard to children's ideas of death through aggression.

Lee: I was 3 when one of my puppies died and it was so strange. We were just playing with this puppy that Lady had, then all of a sudden we had to go to church, and when we came home, there is the dog splattered on the road.

Group: Oh brother! Gee whiz! Really?

Counselor: And you can remember that far back because it was a shock to you?

Lee: Sally started screaming and crying.

Counselor: Sally cried?

Lee: Yeah, that was her favorite puppy.

Counselor: I see. (*Long silence.*) Tom?

Tom: Well, uh, let's see. It was a dog. We had a black dog. We named it Queen, and we was gone somewhere and we came back, and, uh, somebody had run over it, and picked it up and closed the door, and, uh, we go home, and I ran and opened up the door and said, "I wonder who let the dog in?" You know, because it looked like it was sleeping, it hadn't busted any skin or anything.

Counselor: Looked like it was asleep?

Tom: Yeah and, uh I started to wake it up, you know, and it wouldn't wake up, and then I saw it—I just knew something was wrong. It wouldn't wake up and it wouldn't even move. I just lifted up its arm and it just dropped down. Then the others came and they knew it was dead so they—(*Silence.*)

Counselor: Did they say, "It's dead"?

Tom: No. They just told me to go in the house.

Counselor: They didn't explain what had happened to your dog, that it was dead?

Tom: No.

Counselor: But you can remember wondering. You knew it wasn't asleep?

Tom: Uh-huh.

Counselor: So what did you feel? How did you finally decide? How did you find out about it?

Tom: Well, at first I was discouraged. I didn't know what was going on. Finally, George told me.

Counselor: So your older brother finally told you it had died?

These two boys are expressing a common attitude of children toward death as deprivation. Their dead pets didn't move; therefore, the atmosphere of disaster was increased by the adults' reluctance to discuss the deaths and explain the meaning of the stillness in their pets. Without factual explanation, acceptance of the

phenomenon was difficult, and dread of the mystery was increased (Bender 1953).

Bill: We had this dog, about that high, (*long sigh*) and we were going to town that day, but there was a big, heavy rain and there was a whirlpool in our "crick." See, we took both of our dogs down there so we could take a look at it. They both jumped into the water, and all of a sudden one dog came up and the other didn't. The other one never came up. (*Silence.*)

Counselor: So you saw your dog drown? Did you see them bring the body out later? (*Shakes his head negatively.*) You never did? Well, what did you think had happened to your dog, Bill?

Bill: Probably drowned.

Counselor: But at the time, did you know that?

Bill: I thought it swam downstream and ran away.

Counselor: You kinda hoped that it got away.

Jerry: What happened, Bill, when your dog jumped into the whirlpool? I mean did you see it? You mean it was twirling around and going ar-ggg-hh? (*Puts hand to throat, stands up and twirls around.*) Poor dog! (*All nervously laugh at Jerry's imitation of the drowning dog.*)

Bill's experience underscores the importance of explaining death to children when a pet dies. Children live in a world laden with verbal uncertainties and seek to grow from the solid feelings of their senses to abstract generalizations about life and death. The task of making observables and unobservables into a consistent whole is never solved completely even by the adult, but a portion of ideas about death must be based on sound observation if children are to integrate and organize their thoughts and feelings. The group attempted to relieve tension created by this description of death by acting-out behavior and laughing.

Relating experiences about their pets' deaths seemed to give the boys courage to ask questions about their own bodies and possible death. Jerry asked, "What keeps them running?"

Lee answered. "God." (Long silence in the group.)

The boys shied away from discussing religion; that would bring them closer to adult conclusions. Jerry broke the silence with the matter-of-fact remark that some people donate their bodies to scientists who "hang you by your hair and cut your skin open to look inside you and stuff." Jim contradicted him, explaining that an autopsy helped scientists find out why the body stopped running. This comment brought out feelings and stories of when they had thought they were dying, each boy describing vividly the memory of gasping for air.

Lee: Like one time, Sam and Dad and me were playing baseball and I was pitching one and Sam hit one right into my chest. It knocked the air out of me, and I couldn't get my breath and I thought—.(*Silence.*)

Counselor: You really felt you were dying, didn't you?

Jerry: Once, you know I didn't know how to swim, and this kid goes, ''C'mon, let's go out to the 12-foot water and let's fight, and I go, ''Well, I don't want to!'' Then he says, ''Chicken!'' because he didn't care! (*Silence.*) Wish I could have drowned and my mom could have sued him! It makes me sick. I could have shot him! I was mad! (*Giggles are heard from the other boys.*)

His aggression is easily converted into desires of self-destruction, which are stronger than his fears of dying. As Bender (1953) points out, for the young child death does not appear as the natural end of life as much as it is the result of the hostility of others. We see that this attitude is evident from Jerry's feelings about the event.

Counselor: What do you think happens, Bill, when people die?

Bill: They kill you.

Counselor: Who kills you?

Bill: Well, it just seems like little people, (*others in the group snicker*) like Mom, uh, my baby-sitter would say ''God just wanted them up there so He came down and took their life.''

Bill's comments about adult teachings indicate that even at 11 years of age children are not bothered by contradictions. In general, children find it difficult to incorporate conventional, metaphysical, and religious experiences into their own experiences (Bender 1953). Our group discussions brought out a great many feelings, factual distortions, and memories of the children that, at the time, were not well integrated nor explained.

Conclusion

Two years have passed since these meetings, and recently the same children approached me as 13-year-old boys who faced high school. They seemed to have forgotten our earlier conversations about death, until one boy told me of the recent death of his grandfather. As he shared his story and was questioned about the death, tears came to his eyes and he cried gently without embarrassment. His friends were quiet and contained. They discussed their feelings and expressed the fact that they didn't feel afraid anymore and that the meetings

had helped them. The conversation then took a natural turn to sports and girlfriends.

I realized that as a counselor I had been privileged to witness their growth towards an understanding of dying. I felt that in developing their concept of death, they had achieved a measure of intellectual maturity that marked the beginning of their need to reach toward the kind of sensitivity and acceptance of the unknown mysteries of life upon which they could build social and emotional maturity.

For them the ''conspiracy'' of silence about death had seemed to be broken, and it is hoped that they will continue to grow toward adulthood able to face their own deaths with courage. As awareness of death is integrated into individual consciousness, health will be restored to our society. Recognition that life is a precious gift can be encouraged, and manifestations of the creative life energy in all its forms will be accepted and nourished for future generations.

References

Alexander, I. E., & Adlerstein, A. M. Affective responses to the concept of death in a population of children and early adolescents. *Journal of Genetic Psychology,* 1958, *93,* 167–177.

Anthony, S. *The discovery of death in childhood and after.* New York: Basic Books, 1972. (Originally published as *The child's discovery of death.* Harcourt, Brace, 1940).

Bascue, L. O., & Krieger, G. W. Death as a counseling concern. *Personnel and Guidance Journal,* 1974, *52,* 587–592.

Bender, L. *Aggression, hostility, and anxiety in children.* Springfield, Ill.: Charles C. Thomas, 1953.

Berg, C. D. Cognizance of the death taboo in counseling children. *School Counselor,* 1973, *21,* 28–32.

Fulton, R. (Compiler). *Death, grief, and bereavement: A bibliography 1845-1972.* (3rd ed.) Minneapolis: Center for Death Education and Research, University of Minneapolis, 1973.

Gordon, A., & Klass, D. Goals for death education. *School Counselor,* 1977, *24,* 339–347.

Kübler-Ross, E. *On death and dying.* New York: Macmillan, 1969.

Kutscher, A. H., & Kutscher, M. (Compilers). *A bibliography of books on death, bereavement, loss, and grief: 1935–1968.* (Supplement 1968–1972). New York: Health Sciences, 1974.

Mahler, M. S. Helping children to accept death. *Child Study,* 1950, 98–99; 119–120.

Mills, G. C.; Reisler, R.; Robinson, A.; & Vermilyne, G. *Discussing death: A guide to death education.* Homewood, Ill.: ETC Publications, 1976.

Mitford, J. *The American way of death.* New York: Simon & Schuster, 1963.

Nagy, M. The child's theory concerning death. *Journal of Genetic Psychology,* 1948, *73,* 3–27.

Nelson, R. C., & Peterson, W. D. Challenging the last great taboo: Death. *School Counselor,* 1975, *22,* 353–358.

Reisler, R., Jr. The issue of death education. *School Counselor,* 1977, *24,* 331–337.

Schilder, P., & Wechsler, D. The attitudes of children towards death. *Journal of Abnormal and Social Psychology,* 1934, *45,* 406–451.

Stanford, G., & Perry, D. *Death out of the closet. A curriculum guide to living with dying.* New York: Bantam, 1976.

Wolfenstein, M., & Kliman, G. (Eds.). *Children and the death of a president.* New York: Doubleday, 1965.

Section II
Instructional Methods

School Management of the Seriously Ill Child

by David M. Kaplan, Aaron Smith, and Rose Grobstein

The seriously ill child of school age poses difficult management problems for school administrators and teachers who are responsible for the education and health of their children. School teachers and administrators can meet the needs of all their children more effectively if they become aware of their own reactions to serious illness and understand how these personal responses may prejudice the judgments and decisions they must make on behalf of the seriously ill child. The child's ability to cope with a serious illness is largely dependent on the behavior of adults in his immediate environment.

The observations of school management of the seriously ill child cited in this paper were drawn from a study of the impact of childhood leukemia on families.[1] Since many of the study children were of school and preschool age, we were in a position to note incidents involving these seriously ill children at school. Along with family members and health personnel, the school teacher and the classroom situation are of considerable importance to the seriously ill child.

The management and policy issues raised by the seriously ill child for school personnel include the following: How can the school best provide for the special needs of the seriously ill child? How much of the answer lies in separate schools and separate classes for the chronically sick or disabled child? How can the school meet the needs of the normal child vis-a-vis the seriously ill child? Should well classmates be regularly exposed to the seriously ill child? What are the psychological effects of mutual exposure on both groups of children?

How should the school deal with the feelings, requests and demands of both groups' parents? How can school personnel be helped in their reactions to the seriously ill child? How should questions about illness from children, including the seriously ill child, be answered? What information about the illness is confidential and what is properly disseminated to the seriously ill child, his classmates, parents and teachers?

While there is no simple formula to follow in resolving these problems, it is important that the search for solutions take place in a favorable climate, *i.e.*, in an atmosphere in which decisions concerning the seriously ill child are not prejudiced by the decision-maker's own difficulty in coping with serious illness as an eventuality for himself and those he cares about.

Two assumptions are made in this report. The first is that the seriously ill child by virtue of his illness belongs to a minority who, inadvertently, threaten healthy people, making them feel anxious and uncomfortable, largely because the very sick remind us of our own vulnerability. These unpleasant feelings are successfully repressed as long as we can avoid contact with the seriously ill child. The second assumption is that normal adults who have not come to terms with serious illness, and who are required by their work to make decisions concerning sick children, are very likely to protect themselves in situations involving the seriously ill child and, in that process, fail to meet the needs of these children.

PROTECTIVE REACTIONS TO THE SERIOUSLY ILL CHILD

Protective reactions to the seriously ill child which educators may experience are, of course, not peculiar to them. It is a human response common to a large proportion of lay and professional persons in the community. We see these same protective reactions in parents, siblings, neighbors, friends, relatives, doctors, nurses, etc. Fortunately, there are a goodly number of individuals (but still a minority) who have learned through life circumstances to accept their own eventual illness and death. This group is able, by and large, to meet the needs of the seriously ill child without any risk of prejudice to his interests. How can those of us, with responsibility for children, who are, understandably, threatened by the seriously ill child, learn to control our anxiety and discomfort? While the solution to this problem is not easily achieved, becoming aware of protective responses may constitute a first step in the control of such prejudicial actions.

In the study at Stanford Medical Center referred to earlier, 40 families with a leukemic child have been followed from the time the diagnosis of leukemia was suspected and the child was brought for medical attention, through treatment, until three months after the death of the child. One goal of the investigation has been to identify adaptive and maladaptive coping patterns of family members in this situation; another, is to understand the essential nature of both kinds of coping response. It is clear from this study and others like it,[2] that the family's failure to cope in this situation results in a serious weakening of family relationships.

One common response to a threatening minority is to expel these offenders from daily social activities and to remove them from the community, if possible. In this manner, the mentally ill and retarded have been banished from society by committing them to distant state facilities for indeterminate periods. The seriously ill child can also be isolated by his family, while he is in the treatment hospital, by infrequent and brief visits, or by telephoning instead of visiting the patient.

Where long-term expulsion is not feasible, well persons can diminish contacts with the seriously ill child and withdraw emotionally, even in the face of regular contacts. Such reactions from family, friends, health and school personnel are typically rationalized as being in the child's best interest or necessary to protect members of the family or of the community. In fact, such behavior does not benefit anyone. The evidence from the Stanford study of leukemic families indicates, clearly, that the families who suffer most are the ones who seek to protect the child or themselves by withholding information or limiting their contacts with the ill child.

Mr. and Mrs. K. could admit to themselves and others that their three-year-old son had leukemia, but they could not cope with or make the necessary adjustments given that fact. They refused to visit the child when he was hospitalized, stating that it was too hard on him when they left. Mrs. K. claimed she was too ill to drive the distance from their home to the hospital. They couldn't take care of him when he was really sick, so why bother to visit him. They refused to allow their 17-year-old son to visit the ill child because they felt his school work would suffer and he would not be able to graduate with his class. The brother obeyed his parents with much reluctance and stopped visiting the patient, but he continued to express guilt and resentment toward his parents for this restriction. The leukemic child was literally abandoned by his family during hospitalization and no appeal from the hospital staff made any difference in their attitude. The child

became increasingly withdrawn and very frightened during each hospitalization.

The school, as the family, can isolate the child by closing its doors to the seriously ill child, by arranging a school transfer or by limiting the child to a home care teaching program when regular school attendance is medically feasible and advisable.

Mary's diagnosis of leukemia occurred when she was about to enter preschool class in the neighborhood elementary school. Even though her parents tried not to share their knowledge of the diagnosis with anyone, it became common neighborhood knowledge. Several neighbors became concerned that her illness was contagious (there is no medical evidence to indicate that leukemia is contagious) and refused to allow her to play with their children. They became even more alarmed when they learned that Mary was about to begin school with their children. The school was prevailed upon, by these frightened parents, to withdraw Mary's name from the new class list. The school acknowledged its inability to meet the child's needs and in closing the door to Mary rationalized this decision by emphasizing the importance of protecting the other children from the negative psychological effects of exposing well children to Mary on a daily basis and vice versa.

Where expulsion does not occur, teachers can also limit contact and withdraw emotionally from the seriously ill child.

Linda was her teacher's acknowledged "pet," so much so that she had spent some weekends visiting her and her family. The teacher was also a family friend, always available during a crisis. The teacher was the first to observe Linda's pallor and fatigue, and mentioned it to the child's mother who made an immediate appointment with the child's pediatrician. When the diagnosis was made, the family did not share it with anyone, including Linda's teacher. The child returned to school after being absent for three days, her pallor was still evident and the parent's avoidance of the teacher amplified her concerns and suspicions.

Three weeks after the diagnosis, Linda's teacher visited the family and urged them to tell her what was wrong with the child. The impact of the knowledge that it was leukemia overwhelmed the teacher. She wished that she had not become so attached to Linda. Her subsequent avoidance of the child was expressed by her unwillingness to be as involved as she had been in the past with the child or her family. Her aloofness was evident to the child as well as the other children, none of whom understood why. The child became withdrawn, preferring to remain at home and not go to school. The teacher stopped visiting the family and seemingly severed all relationships with the family. Although the teacher and family later managed to resume limited contacts with each other, the relationship never returned to its former closeness and was terminated altogether.

Fortunately, there are many instances in which the teacher and school do act in the best interest of the seriously ill child and of the school.

Mark's teacher was understandably shocked when his mother informed her that he had leukemia. She very quickly recognized that theirs was a close-knit community and it would not be long before everyone would know about Mark's illness. Mark's family discussed his illness very openly with him, feeling the responsibility was theirs and that there would be no secrets about it. Once, when Mark was out of school because of the flu, his teacher acquainted the other children with the fact that Mark was ill, that his appearance would undergo a change, but they were not to be frightened, nor were they to make fun of him. She reminded them of how kind they had been to others of their group who had been ill, and that Mark deserved the same understanding. When Mark returned to school there were no incidents relating to his appearance, even after he lost all of his hair. He missed numerous days away from school, but he enjoyed those days he did attend.

Donna was diagnosed at the age of two, just about the time her mother had intended to place her in nursery school. Donna's mother refused to enroll her after a year had passed, fearing the child would become exposed to viruses her body could not handle. The physicians had recommended that Donna be allowed to relate to other children, but her family continued to resist the idea. The teacher in charge of the preschool program in Donna's neighborhood became aware of the situation, approached the family and convinced them that the school would not be harmful to the child. The school liberalized its admissions requirements and allowed Donna's mother to enroll the child on an hourly basis for several weeks until she felt comfortable enough to leave her on a full-time basis. The teacher's patience and understanding helped the entire family to cope more positively with their feelings about their child's illness. She remained in the preschool program for one and a half years and missed very few days.

In the examples cited, the first teacher was able through open discussions to prevent reactions by well classmates and their families that might have isolated the seriously ill child. In the second illustration, the teacher helped the seriously ill child's family allow the child to get the most out of school, despite her limitations. The benefits of such actions for all those involved are very great.

Separating and withdrawing from those who threaten us is a common method of self-protection. Another frequent protective response is to refuse to believe the facts of serious illness, to pretend that all is well or will work out well. With many seriously ill children, all is not well and is not likely to get better. Parents with their considerable stake in a child and his future often refuse to accept the implications of serious illness. These parents avoid those who refer to the illness as "leukemia." They do not use the term themselves, but substitute euphemisms in speaking of the child's illness. In some cases the parents deny the obvious symptoms of the illness and the results of treatment.

Mr. and Mrs. H. stated that their 15-year-old son was not emotionally strong enough to be told his diagnosis. When the child asked his parents what was wrong with him they told him he had a virus, but he would be O.K. When the child expired several months later, his best friend informed the parents that their son knew he had leukemia, but could not tell them he knew.

The face of the once slender and attractive four-year-old son of Mr. R. became puffy and round soon after steroid treatment began. The physical change in the child was obvious to everyone but his father, who when reminded of these changes by his wife, became very angry and would refuse to talk with her for several days. He disclaimed changes in his son's appearance.

School personnel also respond to serious illness in a child with shocked disbelief and the hope that a "miracle" will occur to cure him.

Mrs. T. was extremely proud of Leila, a 12-year-old who had blossomed in her class from a shy child doing average work to one who suddenly caught fire and showed outstanding ability. When Leila's mother tearfully explained recent lethargy, pains and absences due to a diagnosis of leukemia, Mrs. T. paled and almost fainted. However, Mrs. T. rallied quickly, assuring the mother that current research in cancer promised great hopes for Leila. Her teacher became increasingly involved with the child and her family. She urged Leila to continue to exert effort in class to maintain her new standing, bringing assignments home for Leila when her illness kept her from school. Mrs. T., during these visits to the family at home, would not tolerate the mother's tears. She exuded hope and confidence and felt justified when Leila's treatment resulted in an extended remission. During this period, Leila was urged to work toward earning a place in a special school project for bright children.

After several months, Leila suffered a relapse and returned to the hospital for inpatient care. Her teacher took this setback very hard. She felt depressed and found it most difficult to visit Leila in the hospital. Mrs. T. visited twice, but left quickly to control her tears. She failed to attend Leila's funeral several months later. Her teaching suffered during this period; she found herself preoccupied with thoughts of Leila and her death. Mrs. T. paid a brief visit to the family some time after the funeral, but was quite uncomfortable. She has not had any subsequent contact with any member of Leila's family. Two of Leila's younger sisters still attend the same school.

SUCCESSFUL COPING WITH THE SERIOUSLY ILL CHILD

Our study of familial success and failure in adapting to the seriously ill child indicates that outcome is a result of individual and family efforts to cope and is not a fortuitous or foregone conclusion. Those who are able to face and resolve the psychological tasks posed by serious illness are likely to achieve a good outcome. The prototypical adaptive coping reactions can serve as a model for others, *e.g.,* teachers who also become appropriately emotionally involved with their students and have to cope with them when they unexpectedly become seriously ill.

Adaptive coping families are able to understand that leukemia is a serious, ultimately fatal illness involving remissions and exacerbations, but moving progressively toward a terminal state. This realistic understanding of the illness and of what it holds for the future is not arrived at without considerable anguish. These parents must reach a number of painful realizations. They must accept having a chronically, seriously ill child in place of a normal child, which conception is a necessary prelude to making those changes in living that a very sick child requires. The realization that a child, who was considered healthy until recently, is seriously ill is, in itself, an occasion for family mourning. The further recognition that there is no cure or good prospect of long-term survival adds to the shock and grief these parents experience initially in anticipation of the eventual loss of their child.

It is of considerable importance for both parents to communicate the true nature of the illness to the family. At the outset it is sufficient for them to convey to all members of the family that the leukemic child suffers from a serious illness that will require regular and continuous medical care. Medical care is aimed at returning the child to his home in remission.

The communication of the nature of the illness in the family is accompanied by a grief period which involves all members. The diagnosis ushers in a phase of shared family mourning and mutual consolation that includes the leukemic child.

Family mourning is not completed at the outset, but may extend over a long period as an intermittent process in which all members participate. There are many losses associated with serious illness in a child, *i.e.,* goals that must be relinquished forever and other values that must be postponed indefinitely. Teachers also become emotionally involved with their students and look forward to the normally rewarding experience of participating in and following the educational and personality development of their students. When a teacher learns of serious illness in a child, she goes through essentially the same process as the parent. Teachers experience shock, disbelief, anger and a sense of loss that is a normal reaction to such unhappy news.

Teachers, like parents, must also learn to accept serious illness in a child who previously appeared to be normal, healthy, and able to engage fully in school pursuits of all kinds. There are immediate losses the teacher must face, *e.g.,* frequent absences, a slowing down in usual learning and growth patterns, possible failure to advance normally, changes in physical appearance. Long-term losses include failure to finish school or to participate in extramural activities, physical deterioration, disability, and, finally, death.

SCHOOL MANAGEMENT ISSUES

While school arrangements for the seriously ill child must be considered in terms of the individual needs of the child, decisions to separate the seriously ill or disabled child from well classmates should be carefully reviewed to be sure that the decision is based on the needs of the child and not on adult protective considerations, either explicit or implicit. Children are not likely to be damaged by exposure to reality, however unpleasant it may be. Our experience indicates that adults have a far greater concern for such harm than the facts warrant.

The feelings and wishes of anxious parents must be given due consideration, but again, requests to isolate the seriously ill child or to keep him from regular school attendance that are based upon unsubstantiated claims that the well children may be harmed by such contacts should be treated as the facts indicate. The examples we have cited indicate that the members of the community will respond to the school's leadership in such matters as long as the fact about illness are presented to them and they are given an opportunity to separate fact from fantasy.

The dissemination in the school of information about illness, including serious ones, can be accomplished effectively when this information is imparted by adults who are themselves concerned for the child but not overwhelmed by his illness or its prognosis. The seriously ill child's own questions about his health can also be handled by school personnel without fear of inadvertently precipitating a crisis. Most seriously ill children have a good idea of the seriousness of their illness. Questions about their health usually indicate that they have had problems in getting accurate answers from their parents or from health personnel. The teacher can be most helpful by asking the child for his own understanding of his illness and following the discussion by offering to take up the question with the child's parents, if this seems needed.

Those teachers and other school personnel who are able to face the painful realities of serious illness, to experience the loss and sorrow involved, are likely to be of greatest help to the seriously ill child in his school experience. The importance, to the seriously ill child and his family, of the child continuing to find satisfaction and fulfillment in school cannot be overestimated. The value, to the rest of the school, classmates, teachers, and parents, of seeing the seriously ill child participate meaningfully in school is also difficult to measure. There can be no doubt that many normal children and adults will learn to approach serious illness in their own lives more effectively as a result of witnessing a demonstration in the school of what can be done to help these children.

REFERENCES

1. Kaplan DM, Smith A, Grobstein R et al: Family mediation of stress. Social Work 18:4 (Jul) 1973.

2. Bozeman MF et al: Psychological impact of cancer and its treatment. III. The adaptation of mothers to the threatened loss of their children through leukemia, part I. Cancer 8:1–20 (Jan-Feb) 1955; Hamovitch MB: The Parent and the Fatally Ill Child. Duarte, California, City of Hope Medical Center, 1964; Binger CM et al: Childhood leukemia: emotional impact on patient and family N E J Med (Feb 20) 1969, pp. 414–417.

Death Education: A Living Issue

by William L. Yarber

We live in a death-denying society. Despite the fact that death is an inevitable and natural part of the life cycle, it remains a taboo topic. Not only do many parents attempt to shield their young from the events of dying and death, but discussions at church tend to center on the theological, and treatments in the popular media are at best unrealistic. As a result, today's young are growing up with a confused and unnatural image of death.

Many teachers, however, feel that if education is to prepare our children for life, then it should also prepare them for death. They do not advocate that death education in the classroom take the place of discussion at home or in church. But recognizing that educational voids do exist, they see death education as a legitimate vehicle for helping children resolve their feelings about death, in the same way that the schools have entered into sex education. Supporters of death education see the curriculum as emphasizing that we can live life to the fullest only after we accept the inevitability of our own death, with the hoped for end result being increased communication about death—with peers, parents, and the dying.

The topic is not now being handled to any significant degree by the schools. In his book, *Teaching Human Beings,* Jeffrey Schrank fantasizes that if the dead could return to life they would:

. . . see death hidden from children, the dying isolated from the living, and the schools teaching how to play basketball, solve quadratic equations, and learn who the vice-president in 1898 was. But they would never see the living young learn how to die or even how to live with the certainty of death. [13, p. 175]

Both science and health courses are logical avenues for introducing death education into the curriculum. The purpose of this article is to provide resource information for educators interested in developing a death education unit. Suggestions include content areas, guest speakers, other learning opportunities, and films.

Straightening out the teacher

But prior to classroom discussion, the teacher must first confront his or her own feelings about death. As one teacher exclaimed, "Before I can teach children about death, someone has to straighten me out." [4] In *Death Education as a Learning Experience,* Loren Bensley presents five criteria for teaching death education:

1. The teacher must have come to terms with his or her own death feelings, and have admitted not only its [death's] existence, but its full status in the dynamics of his total personality.

2. The teacher needs to know about . . . death education in order to teach it.

3. The teacher needs to be able to use the language of death easily and naturally, especially in the presence of the young.

4. The teacher needs to be familiar with the sequence of developmental events throughout life, and to have a sympathetic understanding of common problems associated with them.

5. The teacher needs an acute awareness of the enormous social changes . . . in progress and of their implications for changes in our patterns of death-related attitudes, practices, laws, and institutions. [1, p. 4]

The importance of the teacher's own attitude toward death and his or her preparation for teaching the subject cannot be overemphasized. Valuable references are listed at the end of this article.

No dearth of content

Few subjects are as intrinsically interdisciplinary. Medicine, law, sociology, psychology, religion, biological science—each offers areas that could comprise a unit on death. Topics chosen and depth of content will depend upon factors such as the interest and maturity of students, and resources and time available. Possible areas of study include:

- Definitions, causes, and stages of death
- The meaning of death in American society
- Cross-cultural views and practices related to death
- The life cycle
- Funeral ceremonies and alternatives
- Bereavement, grief, and mourning
- Cremation
- Cryogenics
- Organ donations and transplants
- Suicide and self-destructive behavior
- Extending condolences to a relative or friend
- Religious viewpoints of death
- Legal and economic aspects of death
- Death portrayed in music and literature
- Understanding the dying relative or friend
- Preparing for death
- Euthanasia

For additional topic areas, including subunits with behavioral objectives and activity suggestions, the reader is referred to Joan McMahon's article, "A Unit for Independent Study of Death Education." [10]

Guest speakers

The many angles from which to approach the subject invite the utilization of community resource persons. Moreover, participation by a variety of persons can be a key factor in enhancing community acceptance of a death education curriculum. Suggested speakers and topics are:

1. Attorney—preparation of a will; legal aspects of death
2. Cemetery or memorial gardens director
3. Clergy—representatives from major religious groups
4. Coroner—determination of death
5. Funeral director—preparation for the funeral; the service; cremation
6. Monument salesman
7. Physician—determining when death occurs; explaining a death to the family; organ transplants
8. Psychologist or psychiatrist—psychological aspects of death; bereavement, grief, and mourning; coming to terms with the death of a relative or close friend
9. Representative from a memorial society
10. Representative from a euthanasia organization
11. Representative from the state medical society—donation of body to the state medical school
12. Representative from an organization dealing in donations of body organs

Learning opportunities

Samples of student learning activities are presented below. Numerous others can be developed by the teacher and students. For over 50 activities applicable to death education in secondary schools, I recommend the text *Discussing Death: A Guide to Death Education.* [11]

Field Trips: A visit to a funeral home can aid in preparing the student to better deal with the death of a close friend or relative. Also, the intense emotion that usually accompanies such a visit will not be present during a school visit. Other possible field trips include a cemetery, crematorium, memorial gardens, or nursing home for the elderly. The educational value of the trips is enhanced if the visit is coordinated with a classroom presentation by a resource person.

Role-playing: Role-playing allows students to draw upon the major concepts of death while preparing them to cope with various situations. Both teacher and student can participate in creating evocative situations. Examples of role-playing situations are:

- A dialogue between a doctor and a teenage patient who is dying of leukemia [2, p. 50]
- A father explaining the death of his wife to his two children, ages 6 and 15 [2, p. 51]
- A teenager going to a funeral home to see a classmate whose parent died unexpectedly [11, p. 85]

Value Clarification: Activities designed to help students clarify how they feel about life situations have become increasingly popular in schools. Sidney Simon and Joel Goodman have developed a set of activities which examine death in a positive and meaningful way. In one, students are given the outline of a six-segmented coat of arms and are asked to draw pictures or symbols in each segment in response to personal questions about life and death. [14]

Planning Own Funeral: This activity requires the individual student to consider the type of funeral that he or she would desire. Students are asked to plan their own funeral as if they were to die soon, in middle-life, or old age. A sample funeral instruction form can be found in Earl Grollman's book *Concerning Death: A Practical Guide for the Living.* [5]

Numerous learning packages and films have recently been produced. Samples of those applicable to the secondary level appear in the accompanying box. The text by Mills *et al.* lists additional media sources. [11]

******

Death education in the schools is not something to be hurriedly initiated without adequate preparation. Properly instituted, however, a program can aid all of us in finding peace with the idea of our own death.

References

1. Bensley, Loren B. *Death Education as a Learning Experience*. ERIC Clearinghouse on Teacher Education, Washington, D.C. 1975.
2. Berg, David W. and George G. Daugherty. *Perspectives on Death: Teacher's Resource Book*. Educational Perspectives Associates, DeKalb, Ill. 1972.
3. Green, Betty R. and Donald P. Irish, editors. *Death Education: Preparation for Living*. General Learning Press, Morristown, N.J. 1971.
4. Grollman, Earl A., editor. *Explaining Death to Children*. Beacon Press, Boston, Mass. 1967.
5. ———. *Concerning Death: A Practical Guide for the Living*. Beacon Press, Boston, Mass. 1974.
6. Hendin, David. *Death As a Fact of Life*. W. W. Morton and Company, Inc., New York, N.Y. 1973.
7. Kübler-Ross, Elizabeth. *On Death and Dying*. Collier-Macmillan, New York, N.Y. 1968.
8. ———. *Questions and Answers on Death and Dying*. Collier Books, New York, N.Y. 1974.
9. Langone, John. *Death is a Noun*. Little, Brown and Company, Boston, Mass. 1972.
10. McMahon, Joan D. "A Unit for Independent Study of Death." *School Health Review* (Now *Health Education*) 4:27–34; July–August 1973.
11. Mills, Gretchen C. *et al. Discussing Death: A Guide to Death Education*. Educational Perspectives Associates, DeKalb, Ill. 1976.
12. *Science for Society, A Bibliography, Sixth Edition*. American Association for the Advancement of Science, Washington, D.C. 1976. (Annual bibliographic series contains section on aging and death with mini-course outline.)
13. Schrank, Jeffrey. *Teaching Human Beings*. Beacon Press, Boston, Mass. 1972.
14. Simon, Sidney B. and Joel Goodman. "A Study of Death Through the Celebration of Life." *Learning* 4:70–74; March 1976.

Learning Packages/Films

- *Death and Dying: Closing the Circle* (3-part sound filmstrip). Guidance Associates, 757 Third Ave., New York, NY 11232. Purchase price $64.50.
- *Living with Dying* (2-part sound filmstrip: *Immortality and Acceptance*). Sunburst Communications, 12 Upper Barnwell Dr., Pound Ridge, NY 10576. Purchase price $45.
- *Perspectives on Death* (4-part sound filmstrip: *Funeral Customs Around the World, Death Through the Eyes of the Artist, Death Themes in Literature, and Death Themes in Music*. Also includes a student activity book, textbook, and teacher's resource book.) Perspectives on Death, P.O. Box 213, DeKalb, IL 60115. Purchase price: $55 for audiovisual package: $2 for teacher's resource book; $2.50 for textbook; $1.50 for student activity book.
- *How Could I Not Be Among You?* (by Thomas Reichman, 16 mm color, 29 minutes. Portrait of a poet who knows he is about to die from leukemia.) The Eccentric Circle, P.O. Box 4085, Greenwich, CT 06830. Purchase price $390; rental $35.
- *You See, I've Had No Life* (by Ben Levin, 16 mm color, 32 minutes. Documentary of a family facing the death of a 13-year-old family member.) Available from The Eccentric Circle, P.O. Box 4085, Greenwich, CT 06830. Purchase price $290; rental $29.
- *Soon There Will Be No More Me*. (by Lawrence Schiller, 16 mm color, 10 minutes. Personal testimony by a young mother facing death.) Available from Churchill Films, 622 North Robertson Blvd., Los Angeles, CA 90069.

A Unit on Death for Primary Grades

by Toni Dahlgren and Iris Prager-Decker

Teaching about death in grades 1 through 3 is a new idea, but many writers, experts in a variety of fields, think it is a good one. This unit is designed to answer some of the questions that children have about death. Ideally, children feel free to discuss their feelings and experiences, so it is likely that a responsive teacher might move into areas not included in the unit. The keys to good teaching in this unit are the same for good teaching anywhere: honesty, naturalness, sensitivity.

There are many ways to approach the subject of death. Poetry and music are excellent avenues. Field trips, speakers, and role-playing meet the needs of the older student. However, for young students, children's literature was chosen as a vehicle to open discussion. Lessons were kept short and the entire unit is only five days—taught in one school week or once a week for five weeks. It should be taught gently.

Activity 1—Basic concept: every living thing dies.

Objectives: The students will distinguish between living and nonliving things. The students will describe how a living thing is different after it dies.

Materials: A living flower planted in a pot, an identical flower which has been uprooted and is dry and faded.

Time: 15 minutes.

Procedure: Ask students—What living things are in this room (plants, pet, students, teacher)? What things in this room are not living (desks, blackboard)? Is water living? Is the sky living? Is lightning alive? Is a teddy bear alive? Or a doll? (We sometimes pretend they are, but they aren't really.) Is a rock alive?

What does a living flower look like? (Hold up the flower.) How is a dead flower different? (Hold up the dead flower.) What does a living bird look like? What does a dead bird look like?

Do you think that each living plant will someday die? Will each animal someday die? Will each person someday die? Every living thing must die. It is a natural part of life.

Evaluation: Some young children are confused about what is living and what is not living. Those who don't have this basic understanding will have special difficulty with the concept of death. Don't push children to understand more than they are ready to understand, but listen carefully to comments and questions so you will know their level of understanding.

Children may introduce comments about their own experiences which don't fit into the subject of this first lesson. Be flexible. Begin now to establish an atmosphere of honesty and a willingness to discuss what a child needs to discuss.

Activity 2—Basic concept: death is final and this makes it very sad.

Objectives: The students will listen to their teacher read The Dead Bird. The students will discuss the book and the "death" of cartoon characters and TV actors.

Materials: The Dead Bird by Margaret Wise Brown (Addison-Wesley, 1958).

Time: 20 minutes.

Procedure: Introduce the book—yesterday we said that every living thing must die. Sometimes we see animals which have died in the woods or in the roads or even in our yards. Have you ever found a dead animal? This is the story of a group of children who found a dead bird.

Read the book.

Ask the students: How did the children in the book know that the bird was dead? How do you think the bird may have died? (It might have been very old; it might have been hurt; it might have had a serious disease.)

Why were the children so sad? (The bird would never fly again and the funeral was sad; they were saying goodbye to a bird which had been alive.)

Would the bird ever be alive again?

Discuss the way characters "die" in cartoons and the way actors die on TV. Do they really die? (Television deaths in stories and cartoons are just pretended. That's why they can come back again and again.)

Can any living thing which has died come back and be alive again? (No, death is final. That's why it is so sad. After you visit your grandmother it is sad to say goodbye, but you know you will see her again. If your grandmother dies and you know you will never see her in her house again, you are very much sadder.)

Did the children in this book really love the bird? (Not really. The bird was not a pet and not a part of their lives.) The book tells us that the children eventually forgot the bird. Is that alright? (Yes, since the children weren't deeply hurt by the death of the bird, their sadness went away quickly.)

Evaluation: Some children may tell you that "Jesus came back from the dead" or "I will see my grandmother in Heaven." There is no reason to contradict these statements in an effort to be scientific. Death is a mysterious and emotional subject—the teacher's main objective is to create a climate in which children can express themselves freely. The point may be made that when someone we love dies we will never see him or her on earth again.

Children often wonder what causes death. Discussing how the bird may have died can be generalized to all living things.

Activity 3—Basic concept: many feelings are experienced in grief.

Objectives: The students will discuss how Ben felt when his dog died. The students will discuss several feelings which might be part of grief.

Materials: *The Old Dog* by Sarah Abbott.

Time: 20 minutes.

Procedure: Introduce the book—yesterday we read a story about a dead bird and we said that the children who found it were sad, but not too sad. What if it were your dog who died? This story is about a little boy named Ben and about the death of his dog.
Read the book.
How did Ben feel when his dog died? What did he do? Was it alright for his mother to cry about the dog? Would it be alright for his father to cry? (Yes, sometimes crying helps to get the hurt out.)

Tell the students: When Ben's dog died, he felt grief. Grief is the hurt you feel when someone you love dies. Sometimes grief includes many different feelings. Ben might feel angry. Why? Who could he be angry at? What could he do if he were angry? He might be angry because his friend still had a dog or because it wasn't "fair" to lose his dog when he loved her so much and treated her so well. He might not know who to be angry at. He might feel like hitting his pillow very hard over and over. Would that be alright? He might feel like yelling at his mother. Would that be alright?

Ben might feel guilty. He might blame himself for his dog's death. He might think, "If only I had fed her more or petted her more, maybe she wouldn't have died." What could Ben do to get rid of his feelings of guilt? (He could talk to his parents; they would probably tell him that it wasn't his fault at all, his dog died because she was old and it was time for her to die.)

Ben might feel fear. He might be afraid to love another dog, because he wouldn't want to be hurt again. He might be afraid another dog would die too. Do you think it was a good idea for Ben to get a new puppy right away? (Ben probably needed time to get over his grief before he could really love another dog. Grief heals, but it takes time.)

This is concentrated material for children. Keep the pace as relaxed as possible with plenty of time for side trips and comments.

Activity 4—Basic concept: certain activities follow a death.

Objectives: The students will discuss what happens after death to the person and to the person's body. The students will compare the two funerals they have read about. The students will draw two pictures—one of death and one of what happens after death.

Materials: *The Tenth Good Thing About Barney* by Judith Viorst (Atheneum, 1975) and *The Dead Bird.* The dead flower. Paper and crayons for each child.

Time: 25 minutes.

Procedure: Introduce the book—yesterday we read about Ben and his dog. In this book Barney, a cat, dies and the two children in the book argue about where he is now.
Read the book.
Ask the students: Where did Annie think Barney was? Where did the little boy who owned Barney think he was? (In the ground.) What does that mean? How could he become part of the ground?

Take the dry flower and crush it between your fingers over a pot of dirt. Pass it around for the students to see.

Tell the students: No one knows for sure what happens after death; people have different ideas. Some people think that we live in the memories of people who love us; some think that we return to earth and are born again. We really don't know.

We do know what happens to the body after death. What do we do with the body of someone who has died? What did the boy in the story do with Barney's body? What did the children do with the body of the dead bird? How were the two funerals alike? (Show the books again.)

Why do you think we have funerals? (It gives us a chance to show how much we love the person or pet who died.) Have you ever been to a funeral? Have you ever held a funeral?

Ask the students to draw two pictures—one of death, one of what might happen after death.

Evaluation: The pictures should give the teacher some idea of how the children conceive of death. Young children often personify death and may draw it as a skeleton or scary person. Teachers are usually not well trained in psychologically interpreting children's art, so be cautious about reaching any conclusions. However, the teacher should be sensitive to what feelings the child is expressing through art and especially sensitive to what the child says about the picture. Don't be shy about asking a student, "What is this?"

Don't be afraid to tell children that you don't know what happens after death. Remember the goal is honesty with each other.

Activity 5—Basic concept: people often need help when someone close dies.

Objectives: The students will plan a funeral for a pet. The students will discuss how they would be able to help the children in the stories which have been read.

Materials: None needed.

Time: 20 minutes.

Procedures: Tell the students: We've been talking about death all this week. I wonder if we know a little more about how to deal with death now. Let's pretend that our class pet has died. Do you think we could plan a funeral for him?

Where would we bury him? What would we bury him in? What would we put on his grave? What would

we say about him? What could we do to make his funeral special? How could we show how much we love him and would miss him?

How could we comfort each other? How could you comfort Ben when he was so sad about his dog's death? How could you comfort the boy who owned Barney?

What would you do if you came to class and found me crying because my friend had died? What would you say to me? Can a child comfort a grown-up? What would you want me to say to you if your friend had died?

Review: We have talked about death every day for a week. We said that every living thing must die. We said that death is sad because it is a final goodbye. We said that grief is the hurt that we feel when someone we love dies. We talked about what happens after death. What happens to the person and to his body? Today we talked about how we can deal with death. Are there any questions or is there anything more you would like to share with the class?

Evaluation: The students should be encouraged to realize that we can talk about death to someone who is grieving; we can listen sympathetically; we can hug him or hold his hand; we can do special, kind things for him; we can be patient with him and let him cry or be angry or withdrawn. We can plan or take part in a funeral for someone we love who has died. We can remember how special the person was and how much we love him. The goal of this final lesson is to show the children that we can deal with death in a positive and loving way.

Bibliography

Crase, D. R. and Crase, D. "Helping Children Understand Death," *Young Children*, 32 (November 1976) pp. 20–25.

Fredlund, D. J., "Children and Death from the School Setting Viewpoint," *Journal of School Health*, November 1977, pp. 533–77.

Grollman, E. A., "Explaining Death to Children," *Journal of School Health*, June 1977, pp. 336–39.

Hart, E. J., "Death Education and Mental Health," *Journal of School Health*, September 1976, pp. 407–12.

Koby, I. M., "And the Leaves that are Green Turn to . . . ?" *English Journal*, October 1975, pp. 59–60.

"Learning About Death," *Language Arts*, September 1976, pp. 673–87.

LeShan, Eda, *Learning to Say Good-bye*, New York: Macmillan, 1976.

Wass, H. and Shaak, J. "Helping Children Understand Death Through Literature," *Childhood Education*, November 1976, pp. 80–85.

Yarber, W. L., "Death Education: A Living Issue," *Science Teacher*, October 1976, pp. 21–23.

Puppet Life and Death Education

MARGARET E. RUCKER, LESLIE M. THOMPSON,
and BEN E. DICKERSON

Because they are such effective teaching resources, puppets are an economical and exciting resource for increasing numbers of teachers involved in courses on death education.[1] Even seasoned teachers frequently experience qualms about dealing with some of the more traumatic aspects of death, and puppets help create an aura of informality and anonymity that permits a candid and informative handling of such sensitive topics. In fact, the construction of puppets and the creation of appropriate skits engender excitement, evoke creativity, demand rational thinking, promote an atmosphere for open discussion, and in general afford a unique learning situation.

The use of puppets gives the teacher an opportunity to employ one of the more popular orientations in sociology—dramaturgy. Henslin describes the dramaturgical perspective "as being similar to the theater, with the analysis of behavior focused on the various masks people wear as they try to get their point across in their dealings with others."[2] Emphasis is placed upon role performance. In this kind of learning situation, students are able to construct and adopt roles for particular social settings. Creation of roles helps to appreciate the distinction in the content and style of behavior. A theatrical view of human interaction also makes it less difficult to understand the "multiplicity of selves" and stress that often occurs in the loss of a loved one. Perhaps the students can even begin to develop and cultivate the necessary expertise for identifying and authenticating roles more reflective of themselves in various crisis situations.

Teachers experienced in the use of puppets are enthusiastic about the significant teaching potential of puppets—an enthusiasm undoubtedly derived from the puppet's potential to create an illusion of life, to assume magical power, to come alive, to laugh, to cry, to convey moods, to be mysterious and even to promote thinking. The anonymity of the puppeteer, moreover, frequently permits him to discuss feelings he might otherwise repress. By transferring his thoughts and feelings to the puppet, even a shy person can express his opinions or ask questions. In particular, puppets afford an opportunity to explore beliefs, sentiments, and expectations perhaps too difficult to encounter in any direct fashion. Puppets also help create an informal atmosphere which can open doors to topics normally not discussed, i.e., donation of body parts, self-destruction, and cryogenics. Puppets additionally prove invaluable in providing opportunities to work through social situations not yet encountered by most of the class.

Puppets serve an invaluable function in helping students overcome emotional problems, and certainly death exemplifies one traumatic area to explore. Such situations often get very heavy, but the personality assumed by the puppet can lighten the subject. Puppets, moreover, cannot—like their human counterparts—be embarrassed by displaying ignorance about death or other matters. In general, then, skillful use of puppets allows the teacher to initiate, control, and terminate discussions easily and, at the same time, maintain the appropriate mood.

Because they can be made from materials readily available, puppets afford one of the most economical teaching aids. In addition, a variety of types of puppets are suitable for classroom use. Glove puppets, for example, are controlled by the student's hand inside the puppet. Such puppets can consist of only a handkerchief over the hand, or a more elaborate puppet can be created from two nine-inch by twelve-inch squares of felt, scraps of felt for facial features, and yard for hair. Other kinds of puppets include rod puppets which are supported by one rod, while one or two other rods move the puppet's head up and down. These rods require both hands and sometimes more than one person. Shadow puppets consist of figures cut out of poster board and then held in back of a sheet while a bright light behind the figure casts the puppet's shadow on the sheet. Marionettes are puppets with moveable arms, legs, head, and sometimes a moveable mouth. While much more versatile than the hand puppet, they require much greater talent and skill both to make and to handle. The much smaller finger puppet fits over the finger. These puppets work effectively with a small group gathered around a small stage. Finally, the sock puppet deserves consideration. The sock serves as the head and the body of the puppet; buttons, yarn, and bits of felt provide facial features; and the toe of the sock can be stuffed with cotton or some other material to serve as a head.

Teachers may plan their skits upon the basis of student need, research, and the advice of experts in this subject area. In addition, the teacher should carefully integrate these assignments into the course outline so they will complement the other course work. It is also important to research thoroughly all of the areas to be discussed and to formulate objectives for each assignment. A well-planned skit should introduce the characters and the problem or conflict, develop the problem, and, when possible, solve the problem. The authors would like to suggest that the discussion of death can often best be introduced through impromptu give-and-take sessions with several puppets. The discussion of student experiences with death, and feelings associated with these incidents, can evoke a whole range of topics on which to develop other skits. Thus, the teacher may use this exercise as a valuable source of information for planning the course.

Even without the exercise above, a host of topics suggest themselves for discussion with puppets, but the ensuing suggestions might prove helpful to teachers with little experience in puppetry and with minimal training in death education. A whole series of exercises might focus upon the ways of coping with the death of a close relation or friend. An extension of this assignment would be to plan a skit involving an imaginary trip to a funeral home to make arrangements for a burial. Additionally, the skit might deal with family apprehensions and emotions following the funeral of a close relative. In all of these situations, the students should prepare the skits and provide the interaction. Other skits could investigate such matters as a parent attempting to reassure a teenager who has lost a parent, or explore the possible feelings of a terminal patient. Puppets can be used to explore the expressions of grief as well as such complex topics as suicide, euthanasia, and capital punishment.

The degree to which teachers now integrate death education into their curriculum manifests their awareness of the importance of this topic to the entire family cycle, and it further underscores a healthy willingness to attempt innovative new approaches. The authors believe that puppets afford teachers a unique opportunity to display further their creativity and imagination, for this too little used medium permits the teacher to probe deeply and meaningfully into a difficult subject while minimizing its traumatic impact on all parties. In short, this combination of pedagogical and intellectual innovation will achieve several objectives integral to the study of death education, as well as give professional and personal satisfaction to the teacher and student alike.

NOTES

1. Such courses have proliferated on college and secondary school campuses during the last five years. Literally dozens of books and articles have appeared in print. The following basic works will prove invaluable to any teacher initiating such a course:

D. W. Berg and George G. Daugherty, "Teaching about Death," *Today's Education,* 62 (March 1974), 46-7; D. R. Crase and Darrell Crose, "Live Issues Surrounding Death Education," *Journal of School Health,* XLIV (Feb. 1974), 70-73; R. Fromanek, "When Children Ask about Death," *Elementary School Journal,* 75 (Nov. 1974), 92-7; Margaret E. Rucker, Leslie M. Thompson, and Ben E. Dickerson, "Death Education: The Home Economics Curriculum," *Journal of Home Economics,* 69 (March 1977), 14-18; L. M. Thompson, Ben E. Dickerson, and Melvin H. Wester, "Death: The Role of the Counselor," *Journal, The Texas Personnel and Guidance Association,* 4 (March 1975), 45-50; Herman Feifel. *The Meaning of Death* (New York: McGraw-Hill, 1965); Betty R. Green and Donald P. Irish. *Death Education; Preparation for Living* (Cambridge, Mass.: Schenkman, 1971); Earl Grollman. *Explaining Death to Children* (Boston: Beacon Press, 1967); David Hendin. *Death as a Fact of Life* (New York: Warner, 1974); Robert E. Kavanaugh. *Facing Death* (Los Angeles: Nash, 1972); Elisabeth Kubler-Ross. *Death; The Final Stage of Growth* (Englewood Cliffs, N.J.: Prentice-Hall, 1975); Elisabeth Kubler-Ross. *On Death and Dying* (New York: Macmillan, 1969); Elisabeth Kubler-Ross. *Questions and Answers on Death and Dying* (New York: Macmillan, 1974); Jessica Mitford. *The American Way of Death* (New York: Fawcett Crest, 1963); Robert E. Neale. *The Art of Dying* (New York: Harper & Row, 1971); Edwin S. Shneidman. *Death: Current Perspectives* (Palo Alto, Calif.: Mayfield, 1976); Edwin S. Shneidman. *Deaths of Man* (Baltimore: Penguin, 1974); Gene Stanford and Deborah Perry. *Death Out of the Closet* (New York: Bantam, 1976); Avery D. Weisman. *On Dying and Denying: A Psychiatric Study of Terminality* (New York: Behavioral Publications, 1972); Rose Zeligs. *Children's Experience with Death* (Springfield, Ill.: Charles Thomas, 1974).

2. James M. Henslin, *Introducing Sociology* (New York: The Free Press, 1975), p. 123.

3. For information about puppets see:

Puppetry Journal, 2015 Novem Drive, Fenton, MO 63026; Mabel Barton and Les Barton, *Marionettes: A Hobby for Everyone* (New York: Thomas Y. Crowell, 1948); Louise Cockrane, *Shadow Puppets in Color* (Player's Inc., 1972); Larry Engler and Carol Fijan, *Making Puppets Come Alive* (New York: Toplinger Pub. Co., 1973); Esme McLaren, *Making Glove Puppets* (New York: Boston Player's Assn., 1973); Tom Tichenor, *Tom Tichenor's Puppets* (Nashville, TN: Abingdon Press, 1971).

Teaching About Death

DAVID W. BERG

GEORGE G. DAUGHERTY

☐ **Perspectives on Death. An unusual topic for a** teaching unit? Perhaps. But in today's classrooms, the unusual is becoming commonplace and the usual— *Silas Marner*, diagramming sentences, the War of 1812, *Great Expectations*, and on and on—is being confronted by challenges from students and teachers alike. The quest for relevance, the search for student motivation, the pursuit of ways to spark the curiosity and capture the interest of our new breed of adolescent is uppermost in the minds of most secondary school educators today. We suggest that half the battle is won when students are offered opportunities to come to grips with topics and issues that have real meaning for them.

It was for these reasons that we decided to offer a thematic mini-course on the topic of death to our junior high students at the University Laboratory School of Northern Illinois University in DeKalb. Our experience with this class has assured us that the topic is indeed meaningful and relevant for today's youth.

The original idea and impetus for teaching this course came from the students themselves after several of them had made an illicit excursion into a funeral home. They came to school the next day filled with questions about their adventure — questions which we were hard pressed to answer. When the students requested that we teach a mini-course on death, we agreed to do so.

As we began our research to prepare for the course, several things soon became clear. First, we found that there was a dearth of materials directed toward secondary school students. Accumulating materials suitable for our students became a major task.

Second, we quickly realized that to teach about death was in reality to teach about many things. Death by its very nature involves science and medicine, social studies and sociology, psychology, history, art, literature, music, insurance, and law. Consequently, our course evolved around the theme of viewing death from several perspectives and attempted to weave the various perspectives together in such a way as to shed light on death as an integral part of life itself.

At the beginning of our course, we attempted to determine the attitudes, knowledges, and concerns of our students so that we might tailor the class to suit their expressed interests. After involving them in informal discussions, we asked them to write down any questions they had concerning any aspect of death or death-related topics. Their questions indicated both a desire for specific information and a wide variety of interests:

Do people always die with their eyes open?

Does your blood change color when you die?

How much money does a nice funeral cost?

Are graves always dug six feet deep?

Why are funerals always sad?

How does the funeral director prepare the body for burial?

Why is black always used to represent death?

Some people call a priest or minister when someone dies, but what use is it if the person is dead?

Other questions related to the physical aspects of death, the moral and ethical issues of abortion and euthanasia, and the spiritual and religious aspects of death and afterlife.

In addition to collecting their questions, we asked the students to respond to a questionnaire we had prepared that asked questions such as these:

Do you believe in any sort of life after death?

Do you have any fears or feelings about death or dying? If so, what are they?

What is the purpose behind funerals and burial ceremonies, both in the United States and in other lands?

What is the definition of death?

One question, asked to determine in a less direct way what some of their feelings were about death, was: "How would you explain death to a young child?" One student unconsciously summarized the feelings of many people, young and old alike, when he answered, "I'd tell him it was a horrible thing—and not to worry about it."

As we progressed through the unit, we called on the services of a variety of resource persons in various fields to speak to the class on their areas of expertise. One of the first of these to talk to the class was a local funeral director, who showed a film on the funeral process entitled "Too Personal To Be Private" and then answered innumerable questions about his profession.

Other guest speakers included our school psychologist, an artist, a musician, a lawyer, an insurance representative, a doctor, representatives of the three major religious faiths, and a soldier, who spoke on facing death on the battlefield and on the benefits the government provides for the survivors of those killed in the service of their country.

In addition to listening to these speakers, students developed a frame of reference through numerous background readings—both fact and fiction, prose and poetry—which enabled them to consider the guest speakers' presentations from a more enlightened point of view. Two field trips, one to a funeral home and one to a cemetery, also added to their growing reservoir of knowledge. In conjunction with the field trips, data sheets were prepared to help them record what they saw and draw conclusions from their observations.

The response from the students at the conclusion of the course was overwhelmingly favorable, as was the response from parents, fellow teachers, and members of the community. We believed even more strongly at the end of the course than at the beginning that here was an area which had three of the basic requisites for inclusion in the school curriculum: universality, tremendous inherent interest, and an alarming lack of knowledge.

Educators, psychologists, and philosophers all offer support for the concept of confronting topics such as death within the nonemotional, noncrisis atmosphere of the classroom.

John Goodlad, dean of the College of Education at UCLA, has charged that "much of the subject matter of today's learning is unrealistically narrow and antiseptic." Alvin Toffler, in *Future Shock*, asks, "Why . . . must teaching be organized around such fixed disciplines as English, economics, mathematics, or biology? Why not around stages of the human life cycle: a course on birth, childhood, adolescence, marriage,

career, retirement, death." And Alfred North Whitehead states unequivocally, "There is only one subject matter for education, and that is Life in all its manifestations."

Not too many years ago, dying and death were very much a natural part of the total family life cycle. Families lived together, often with several generations in the same household. The dying process took place within the family circle as did the death itself and the funeral in many cases. Young people were thus enabled to view the processes of dying, death, grief, and bereavement as natural parts of the total life cycle.

This is not true today, because these processes are typically removed from the family experience. In many instances, the act of dying has lost its dignity and normalcy and has become institutionalized, dehumanized, and mechanized—and young people have been excluded from the experience altogether. The resulting void of experience must be filled if society is to retain a proper perspective toward the value of life.

In addition to the accepted fact that knowledge about and preparation for a critical or traumatic event lessens the psychological effects and helps in the recovery process, teaching about death in the classroom has yet another justification. Young people today are placed in a contradictory and seemingly untenable situation. On the one hand, they are faced daily with life-and-death concerns. War, abortion and euthanasia, growing teen-age suicide rates, the entire ecological question, violence in the media, the mounting drug problem—all of these are real problems facing young people today. On the other hand, adults deny them the opportunity to develop a realistic frame of reference through which to draw conclusions and formulate solutions.

If teachers were free to formulate an axiom for subject matter to be included in the curriculum, perhaps such an axiom would be this: Subject matter for today's education must have *universality*, must be intrinsically *interesting*, must be intellectually *challenging*, must have both personal and social *relevance*, and must prepare students for *life*. We believe that teaching about death meets these criteria. □

Criteria for Evaluating Curriculum Materials in Death Education from Grades K–12

by Marianne (Everett) Gideon

The selection of curriculum materials in death education is often a difficult task. Criteria for selection are discussed and suggestions are made so that death educators teaching in elementary, middle and secondary schools will be able to make informed choices when purchasing or using tests, films, and other curriculum materials.

Tools, books, films, lesson plans, and curriculum guides have been friends of teachers ever since each of these items was invented. Teachers in all walks of life, whether they be parents, master craftsmen, or certified professionals, have learned the advantages of using curriculum materials to supplement their personal talents. We all know that not one tool or series of curriculum guides can replace the human quality that exists when one individual helps another learn, but there is a role in all forms of education for supplementary educational materials. What are curriculum materials and what criteria are used to evaluate these supplements to a teacher's personal qualities, abilities, and knowledge?

Definition of Curriculum Materials

The term *curriculum materials* includes a multitude of resources, including curriculum guides, scope and sequence charts, films, lesson plans, bibliographies, resource lists, teacher training materials, students, incidental media (public media), textbooks, and the teacher's edition of the text, reference books, specimens, field trips, tools, workbooks, tests, programmed texts, simulation games, guest speakers, etc. Any experience, piece of hard- or soft-ware, or human resource that helps the learner learn or the teacher encourage learning is a curriculum material.

Need to Evaluate Death Education Curriculum Materials

Most teachers know that learning is encouraged when activity in the learning situation is varied. Many teachers already use films, guest speakers, and other nonlecture techniques. Teachers, generally recognizing their own limitations, seek and utilize help from cur-riculum guides, programmed texts, and other teacher-oriented curriculum materials. Selection of death education curriculum materials is often made in a variety of less than optimal ways: according to which company gives the largest discount on price; personal attachment to a specific text; recommendation from the "experts" or the school board.

Ideally, each death education curriculum material should be evaluated and selected individually. But on what criteria? Of course, the educational goals should be considered. But in this day of limited budgets, cost is also a major consideration. There are several criteria that one should consider prior to purchasing any curriculum materials, especially those that deal with a sensitive topic such as death and dying.

Of course, many evaluation questions can be answered only in a subjective way. Considerations relating to particular features of the intended students' cultural and educational milieus may also figure heavily in some cases. However, I hope that the guidelines suggested below can help an independent reviewer structure his evaluation of death education materials in a way that will clarify the assets and limitations of the materials in question.

Criteria for Evaluating General Death Education Curriculum Materials

A. Multiple Usage
   1. Age groups—Can this "child's" book be useful to older students as well? Is a particular film appropriate for preteens as well as teenagers?
   2. Topics—What issues are addressed in this material? Most materials cover several topics. Can the same film, book, or filmstrip be used to kick off several discussions or raise several issues?

(e.g., euthanasia and the dynamics of family relationships)

   3. Groupings—Would this film, book, etc. be appropriate in a history class as well as a class on death and dying?

B. Accuracy of Information

   1. Is the information outdated or still current?

   2. Was the material written and/or produced by a group with an obvious bias? If so, will that bias be detrimental or helpful for the intended use of the material?

C. Guidelines for Use

   1. Are there suggested warm-up activities to prepare the students for the material?

   2. Are there suggested prerequisites?

   3. Are there suggested objectives?

   4. Are there suggested follow-up activities to help the learner process what has been experienced?

D. References and Bibliographies

   1. Are they available?

   2. Are they written in such a manner that an interested teacher/learner can continue to learn about the topics in the curriculum material?

E. Quality of the Death Education Curriculum Material

   1. Is it technically well produced? Sound clear? Printing appropriate for age and reading level of students?

   2. Length appropriate? Too long and boring? Too short or too much information covered in too little time/space?

   3. Vocabulary appropriate for intended learners and not laden with euphemisms?

   4. Illustrations appropriate? Scary? Nonthreatening, yet not hiding necessary truths? Large print for the young reader?

F. Availability

   1. Can it be rented or borrowed from a public institution or must it be purchased?

   2. Can film footage be replaced?

   3. Is the book in open stock? Does the publisher have good service?

G. Past Use and Results

   1. Has the material been field-tested? Can one obtain results of that testing?

   2. Have reliable persons/reviews recommended it for your purposes?

H. Educational Quality (specifically for texts, curriculum guides, etc.)

   1. Is there a logical scope and sequence?

   2. What is the philosophy behind the death education curriculum material?

   3. For what population was it designed? Inner city? Rural? Teenagers?

   4. Are there guidelines for adapting it to your population, to "special students," to gifted students, to handicapped students?

   5. Is there a summary available?

   6. Does the producer/author suggest means of evaluating the students?

   7. Are suggested lesson plans offered?

I. Cost

Considering today's limited budgets, cost becomes a very powerful tool for evaluating the purchase of any curriculum material. However, if a specific death education curriculum material can serve a multitude of uses over a long time span and speak to various populations, the cost per use can be markedly decreased. In the long run, an expensive initial outlay may be less expensive than numerous small expenditures.

Conclusion

Obviously there are few purely "objective" criteria by which death education curriculum materials can be evaluated. Despite the necessary subjectivity involved, however, orderly assessments can be made on the basis of a clearly delineated set of guidelines. The concrete suggestions outlined in this article will help individual reviewers of death education materials make more informed decisions about the purchase and/or use of specific curriculum materials.

Section III
Classroom Encounters/
Personal Narratives

Scratchy Is Dead

by Alta Fleming Butler

Dear Parents:

A few days ago, the children found Scratchy, our gerbil, dead in his cage. Since then, we have looked at him, talked about his death, made a "coffin" and buried him. The children have been talking and asking questions about Scratchy's death quite often in the last few days. The day-care center staff and I thought it would be helpful to describe how we handled the situation and some of the children's reactions and concerns.

He Was Very Still

Several four-year-olds were the first to find Scratchy. They thought he was sleeping, but he wouldn't wake up when they shook the cage.

One child said, "I think he's dead." I asked the group why, and they said, "His eyes are closed; he won't move." At this point one child began laughing nervously, another began to get all choked up and all four children moved closer to me.

Then I asked them how they thought Scratchy had died. Some of the theories were: "He was sick." "A mosquito bit him and poisoned him." "He was old." "A turtle came and bit him and killed him." We talked about the theories, eliminating the turtle and mosquito because the cage door was closed and it was too cold for mosquitoes. We considered more carefully the other possibilities and I said, "Scratchy is dead. He was very old and he died."

I explained that we shouldn't touch Scratchy with our hands because we didn't know if he had been sick and that we didn't want to get sick from his body. So I used a pencil to touch his body. This helped the children to see that Scratchy was not sleeping, his body was stiff and he couldn't move on his own. The children's comparison between the gerbil and a nearby sleeping mouse readily proved that Scratchy's heart wasn't beating. By this time several other children had come over, and I repeated some of the same questions about Scratchy and reiterated, "Scratchy is dead. He was very old and he died."

First Reactions

Just before lunch we all gathered together and talked about how we had found Scratchy dead. The children's reaction was very much like that of a group of adults who are told of a death. There was disbelief and a feeling of general discomfort. Several children said, "I'm sad," and became all choked up.

We reassured them by saying, "It's all right to be sad. Scratchy is dead. We'll miss him."

Then the children talked to each other and to the teachers for several minutes. In addition to expressing their feelings, some of the children repeated to others several times, "Scratchy is dead." The two-year-olds said his name over and over. The three- and four-year-olds asked when he would wake up. We told them he wasn't sleeping, he was dead, and he wouldn't wake up.

The children wanted to know what we would do with him. We asked what they thought we could or should do. Then they wondered how he died. We said he was very old. A couple of children wanted to know if he would go to heaven. I said, "I don't know. Maybe he will."

During lunch we continued talking about Scratchy. Some of the children stopped by his cage to look at him and used the pencil to touch his body.

When they woke up from their nap time, several youngsters said, "Scratchy is dead" and immediately went to his cage to look at him again. One half-asleep child mumbled, "Don't bury me." We reassured her and all the children and answered their questions much as we had in the morning.

During the afternoon, "playing dead" was a prominent activity, visits to the cage a frequent occurrence. We displayed several books that related specifically to death and read them to individual children or to small groups. Later on, one of the staff talked to all the children about Scratchy's death—what he could do when he was alive that he could not do now. She brought Scratchy's cage over to the children, who were gathered in a circle, and passed it from child to child, giving each one a chance to comment.

Fear and Mourning

The next day, the children repeated many of their questions from the day before. In addition, several of them expressed fears that their parents or they might die. One child inquired, "Scratchy was four years old. I'm four years old. Could I die too?"

We explained that their parents will probably live to be very old. We also said that Scratchy was very old for a *gerbil*, but that people live much, much longer. We talked with them about all the things they will be doing before they are old, like going to elementary and high school and maybe to college; perhaps being a mommy or a daddy themselves; going to work.

Other questions involved Scratchy's feelings. For example: Could he feel the pencil as it touched him? Why couldn't he open his eyes? When would he wake up? What does he eat now? Each time we said, "No . . . Scratchy's dead." Or, "He can't . . . because he's dead."

During our morning group time, the two-year-olds examined Scratchy in his cage. The three-year-olds listened as a story about a dead bird was read to them and then looked at the gerbil again. The four-year-olds were read a story on remembering the good things about a dead cat and then wrote their own book—"Scratchy's Book." The children drew pictures of what they remembered about Scratchy, such as feeding him or watching him sleep. Then I labeled the pictures and stapled them together. It was interesting to see that almost all the four-year-olds drew a picture of the gerbil after he died and said the label should read "Scratchy is dead." [For titles of children's books on death, see the bibliography at the end of this article.]

Proper Burial

That afternoon one of the staff members displayed a shoe box that the gerbil could be buried in. All the children helped decorate it, and Scratchy was placed inside on a bed of cedar chips. Each child then placed something from one of our previous nature walks, such as a leaf, stick, acorn, or pod in the "coffin."

After these preparations, we all walked to a nearby park and found a suitable place to bury him. The children gathered in a circle around the box and said good-bye to their pet. After the box was placed in the hole, each child filled it with handfuls of dirt and covered it with leaves and flowers.

The next morning many of the children arrived talking about Scratchy, his death and burial. We encouraged this discussion and talked together about how we missed him. A couple of children asked if we would get another gerbil. I said that we probably would after a while. We feel that we should wait for the children to work out their feelings first.

Perceptions and Needs

Being aware of young children's developing perceptions of life and death can prepare you for their sometimes puzzling or upsetting reactions. Following are brief descriptions of those perceptions, based on our experience with Scratchy, and literature on the subject, which you may find helpful. [Publications for adults on children and death are listed in the bibliography at the end of this article.]

* Young children can't believe that life can stop.
* They are beginning to understand time and, therefore, don't yet understand the concept of "forever."
* They believe that the dead can come back to life, that death is not permanent.
* They are curious about the dead and often incorporate dying or death in their play.
* They often react to death in what may seem to be inappropriate ways because they have not yet learned how to deal with, understand or show pain and loss.

To aid you in speaking to your children at home about death in general, I want to share some advice on their needs.

1. Children need to learn how to mourn; that is, to go through the process of giving up some of the feelings they have invested in the animal or person and go on with the living, to remember, to be touched by the feelings generated by their memories, to struggle with real or imagined guilt over what they could have done, to deal with their anger over the loss.

2. They need to mourn over the small losses, such as animals, in order to deal better with the larger, closer losses.

3. They need to be informed about a death. If they aren't told but see that adults are upset, they may invent their own explanations or even blame themselves.

4. They need to understand the finality of death. Because abstract thinking is difficult for them, they may misunderstand if adults say that a person or animal "went away," "went to the country" or "went to sleep." If you believe in heaven and want to tell your children about it, it is important to emphasize that they won't see the person or animal again on earth.

5. They need to say good-bye to the deceased by participating in viewings and/or funerals, if only for a few minutes.

6. They need opportunities to work out their feelings and deal with their perceptions of death by talking, dramatic playing, reading books or expressing themselves through the arts.

7. They need reassurance that their parents will take care of themselves and probably won't die until after their children are grown. It is important that they know that sometimes children die, but only if they are

very sick or if there's a bad accident. It's equally important that they understand that almost all children grow up and live to be very old.

8. They need to know that everyone will die some day. It may be hard for adults to be honest about this fact, but if we deny this, children won't be prepared for dealing with death during their lives.

9. They need to be allowed to show their feelings: to cry, become angry or laugh uncontrollably. The best approach is to empathize with their feelings. For example, you might say, "You're sad. You miss Scratchy. Tell me about it."

10. Most important of all, children need to feel confident that their questions will be answered honestly and not avoided and that adults will give them answers they can understand. Adults should take their cues from the children and answer only what they ask.

For Your Information

Following is a bibliography for children and adults. I highly recommend *About Dying,* which has a text for adults plus one for children. We have all the books on hand and more complete bibliographies if you would like to look at them.

CHILDREN'S BOOKS

About Dying by Sara B. Stein (Walker)
The Dead Bird by Margaret W. Brown (Young Scott Books)
My Grandson Lew by Charlotte Zolotow (Harper & Row)
The Tenth Good Thing About Barney by Judith Viorst (Atheneum)

MATERIALS FOR ADULTS

"Books for Children About Death" by Carolyn R. Aradine, *Pediatrics,* Vol. 57, No. 3, March '76
The Discovery of Death in Childhood and After by Sylvia Anthony (Basic Books)
Explaining Death to Children by Earl A. Grollman (Beacon)
On Death and Dying by Elisabeth Kübler-Ross (Macmillan)

If you would like to talk further, please call me and arrange a time for us to meet.

Sincerely,
Alta

When a Student Dies. . . .

Michelle S. Lubetsky

with
Martin J. Lubetsky, M.D.

■ Early in the fall, 13 year old Mary was out of school with "the mumps." Weeks later, after much suffering, she developed a gum infection. In mid-November, the diagnosis was changed. Mary had leukemia. As a second-year teacher of trainable mentally impaired students, I had never before faced a crisis of this magnitude. I began to search for answers for myself as well as for my students.

From my knowledge of the five stages of death and dying as described by Elizabeth Kübler-Ross, I knew that denial would be my first reaction to this tragic news. I was therefore determined to face the facts realistically. It wasn't until much later that I became aware of the ways in which I did, in fact, deny Mary's impending death. I concentrated only on the disease itself, rather than its inevitable consequences. Even when talking with the family, I never permitted any of their foreshadowing to penetrate the barrier.

I found that I had a great need to help in a situation in which I felt helpless. I felt empathy for the parents of all terminally ill children—their fears, their apprehension, and their sense of uselessness as doctors, nurses, and technicians increasingly assume the necessary decision-making roles and eventually become solely responsible for the child's care. Mary's family fought long and hard to have Mary come home from the hospital. Her homecoming was their only solace. They needed to be taking care of Mary as much as she needed them to take care of her.

As my barrier of denial began to retreat, it was replaced by anger. I was angry that an innocent child was to be taken from persons who loved her. I was angry that she was being taken from *me* and that I should have to experience such a trauma. I was even angry at every 13-year-old who was healthy and strong.

Finally, however, I began to accept Mary's fate. Instinctively one day, I took out her notebook and threw it away. When the students questioned me, I answered truthfully that Mary would not be using it any more. After my students had left for the day, I phoned Mary's parents. Mrs. Smith was glad that I had called—Mary had died the night before. She described the final surge of life's energy and the moments before death shared by mother and father, brothers and sisters. I could say nothing. I hung up and cried.

I managed to inform the appropriate school personnel and then was overwhelmed by a sense of panic and confusion. At the request of Mary's family, the parents of my students had not been told that she had leukemia. How was I now to tell them of her death? More distressing, how would I tell my students?

These questions remained unresolved until our school social worker referred me to a friend of hers, who was a grief therapist. We discussed Mary, my students, my fears. She explained that I would not be able to help others understand or cope with this crisis until I was able to accept it myself. She helped me realize that the only proper vehicle of communication was honesty. I had to be genuine in expressing my feelings. My students needed to know that it was all right to feel sad and even to cry. I was their role model. She also stressed that it was important not to treat the family as "lepers." They would need my friendship more than ever.

The next morning I met briefly with our social worker and program coordinator. The three of us then met with the general education students who worked as aides in my classroom. Finally, I returned alone to my classroom to talk with my own students. We gathered our chairs around the record player and talked about our favorite songs. I asked the class whether they remembered Mary's favorite album, and they told me that it was "Annie." As we played the record, we talked about the fact that Mary had been very, very sick. I emphasized the extreme nature of her disease so that the students would not associate *every* illness with death. I asked what might happen if someone was *very* sick. No one offered an answer. "Might that person die?" I probed. We then discussed our own experiences with death. Scott's dog had died, and Howard said that his grandmother had died. I added, "What do you think might have happened to Mary? Yes, she died, too."

Next, I explained that it was o.k. to feel sad, because we loved Mary and would miss her very much. Howard began to cry. I said, "Sometimes we need other people to help us out when we are sad. Do you feel like you might need a hug right now?" We held each other for a moment, and then Howard assured me he would be all right.

Scott's eyes filled with tears as he told us, "We'll get a new Mary." But when questioned, he realized we could not. The other students sat quietly as if in disbelief. They did not understand death, but they understood the sadness.

We wanted to do something to remember Mary, so the class decided to draw pictures. We remembered lots of fun times we had had with our friend, and then we went back to our desks to an array of paper and crayons. I walked around the room and asked the students to explain their drawings. I wanted to keep them, but I felt that it was more important for the students to take them home to give their parents a starting point for discussion. I called each parent so they would know what had happened and could talk about it with their child.

I was now on my way to *acceptance*. There was still one need that I had not yet satisfied: my need to "help" the family. I told myself over and over again that I must call on the Smiths, but I could not bring myself to go. I was, in fact, treating them as "lepers." My visit to their home was the hardest part of the whole experience for me. It was Mrs. Smith who finally asked about the children's reactions to the news, which opened the door to sharing our feelings.

Many school staff members and parents wanted to make contributions to the Leukemia Foundation. My need to help was now channeled into a new direction. I began a fund in Mary's name. We contributed a total of $200 to the Leukemia Foundation, and a plaque was prepared for our school in memory of Mary. The plaque reads, "Let me win, but if I cannot win, let me be brave in the attempt. In loving memory of Mary Smith, January 16, 1980." The quotation is the theme of the National Special Olympics, in which Mary had participated.

In helping to guide my students through a tragedy, I also learned to cope with my own feelings. I developed a healthier attitude toward death and dying. My students were my counselors, as I was theirs, and Mary's memory is still very much alive in each of us.

RELATED READINGS

Berg, C. D. Helping children accept death and dying. *Personnel and Guidance*, November 1978, *57*, 169–172.

Bryant, E. H. Teacher in crisis: A classmate is dying. *Elementary School Journal*, March 1978, *78*, 232–241.

Dahlgreen, T., & Praeger-Decker, J. Unit on death for primary teachers. *Health Education*, January/February 1979, *10*, 36–37..

Fairchild, T. N. *Counseling exceptional children: The teacher's role*. Austin, TX: Learning Concepts, 1977.

Furman, E. Helping children cope with death. *Young Child*, May 1978, *33*, 25–32.

Gowan, J. C. *The guidance of exceptional children: A book of readings*. New York: David McKay, 1972.

Hanley, D. E. *Guidance and the needs of the special child*. Boston: Houghton-Mifflin, 1975.

Keith, C. R., & Ellis, D. Reactions of pupils and teachers to death in the classroom. *School Counselor*, March 1978, *25*, 228–234.

Kübler-Ross, E. *On death and dying*. New York: MacMillan, 1969.

Teacher in Crisis: A Classmate Is Dying. —————Ellen Huntington Bryant

John's sister had leukemia. She was a year older than he and went to the same school as John. Everyone in John's second-grade class knew who his sister was, even those who didn't know her name. Her name was Anne, but everyone recognized her as the girl who was sick. The children didn't know the name of the disease Anne had, but they knew it was something terrible because no one was supposed to talk about it. John didn't know many details about the disease, but his mother always told him everything was going to be fine. John was confused, however, because she told him with tears in her eyes and a voice that caught in her throat.

One morning, over the loudspeaker, the principal announced a change in the bus schedule and a cub scout meeting. Then he said that he was sorry to tell everyone that Anne Bradbury had died.

The children were stunned at this news. Mrs. Russell, John's teacher, said it was a terrible, terrible thing. She asked them not to mention Anne's name to John when he returned to school because it might upset him. The children wondered to themselves: How did she die? Had she hurt? Where was she now? Stealthily, masking the intensity of their feelings, they slipped a few questions into the beginning discussions of the day. What disease had Anne had? Could they get it? What happened at a funeral? What would happen to her body? How would John act? Mrs. Russell said she wanted all this talk about death stopped; it was time to get on to pleasanter things.

But the discussion did not stop. It simply moved from classroom to playground, where what few facts were known were altered by gossip and speculation.

Meanwhile, in an effort to insulate John from further pain, his parents immediately sent him to visit friends in another state. John perceived that his parents loved Anne more than him. They didn't even want him around! When he asked about Anne's death, he was told that God had chosen her to be with Him. John felt panic. Would God want him, too? John couldn't wait to return to school and feel normal again.

But John didn't feel normal at school at all. There was a barrier between him and his classmates. Rather than risk saying something inappropriate to John, the children simply avoided him. Mrs. Russell and John's other teachers were sympathetic but unsure as to the best way to approach him. They told him life would get better and to try to think about happy things. Three months later, when John's grades had slipped and his mood had darkened, Mrs. Russell said he would just have to get his "chin up" and "buckle down" to work. In the hope of protecting John, Mrs. Russell had isolated him.

John couldn't buckle down to work because his life was in chaos. He could not forget that throughout much of his sister's illness he had wished her dead. Was he responsible for her death? He continued to worry that God would take him or, at the least, punish him. He also knew that things were not right at home; his mother had moved into Anne's room.

Mrs. Russell visited John's mother to express sympathy. With tears in her eyes, John's mother went over the story of Anne's death. She added that she feared that she could not hold up and that she and John's father had no real married life any more. Mrs. Russell was deeply concerned for John's mother and her family, but was also embarrassed and at a total loss as to how to handle the situation. Feeling completely inadequate, she said she was sure that everything would be all right in time and left.

Mrs. Russell wrote in John's file that there might be problems ahead for this family. And there have been. John's parents are separated; John drifts aimlessly through school. For some time John and Anne's classmates were fearful of hospitals, terrified of leukemia, and anxious about death. When they think about Anne and John, they remember not the human qualities and shared experiences, but the forbidden fascination and speculation that surrounded Anne's death.

John goes to school in a district where I taught. This situation deepened my concern over the problems that arise when death comes into the lives of children in elementary school. My inquiries led me to Lynwood Swanson, chaplain and director of the Department of Pastoral Care at the Wilmington Medical Center in Wilmington, Delaware, and chairman of the Delmarva Ecumenical Agency responsible for the development of chaplaincy programs in nursing homes and institutions. From him I hoped to gather information that might be helpful to classroom teachers facing a crisis in the family of a pupil.

A teacher needs to know what the family of a dying child is experiencing and should be aware of the fears and the concerns of that child's classmates. An understanding teacher can make a dramatic difference in the ability of a family or an individual to cope with such a crisis.

Parents in crisis

A teacher can have a dramatic role as a member of the health-care team when a child in her class is facing death, for the teacher's world extends beyond the four walls of the homeroom. Her concerns include the relationship between the parents and the child. A crisis that affects one family member affects the interaction of many family members. A teacher needs to know the various stages and attitudes experienced by a family in crisis.

Suspicion that there is a problem is generally the first fear on the part of the parents. The suspicion may be roused by a single event, such as a seizure or a sudden motor malfunction, or perhaps a series of occurrences suggesting a chronic problem. Panicked, the parent and the child (if older than six) wonder what is happening. The body, which has been taken for granted as sound and healthy, is suddenly seen as unreliable. Suspicion takes on stark reality as the event recurs or as the problem becomes more evident.

Tests begin, and the waiting starts. The parents are fearful of what might be found; every possible disease is imagined. Waiting-room stories abound, random reading sparks new fears. Well-meaning friends and relatives press close with suggestions of other doctors, other hospitals, and undermine whatever confidence the parents have in their own course of action. The parents become frustrated and are troubled. If there is difficulty in reaching the doctor, the parents feel that the doctor doesn't care. Time passes slowly, and Mother, who sits in the hospital with the child all day, wonders whether anything is really being done. Other consultations are sought, increasing both expectation and fear. The parents dread loss of control; tests and procedures used on their child are totally out of their hands. The child wants to go home; his tearful pleading adds to the parent's sense of inadequacy and frustration. This period of waiting stretches interminably; the family feels desperately helpless.

The fears become specific when the diagnosis is made; but at the same time there is a sense of movement, for now treatment is underway; procedures are being used; hope has a focus. In the early stages of treatment there is an upswing in mood. Remissions give encouragement.

But the parents are desperate. Routine requirements of the everyday world are unrelenting. Bills must be paid. Phone calls must be made. Breadwinners must go to work. The other children in the family must be taken care of. Inside the parents, private voices scream: "Help! Doesn't anyone know? My life has stopped! Doesn't anyone realize the seriousness of the situation! Part of me is dying!"

At this point the parents' desire to manage the situation is more intense than at any other time. Books about the disease are read, the slightest change in treatment or condition is challenged, hospital routines are questioned. The parents feel desperately out of control. The hospital has usurped all physical aspects of parenting. The parents are concerned about their ability to cope. They wonder how their other children will be affected. They experience financial constraints. They fear the child's death and wonder how he will die. There is pain as they see their child realize that his parents are not omnipotent; they are powerless to protect him. Between husband and wife, there is great concern for the other's ability to cope with such pain.

As death approaches, there is resignation, seldom acceptance. This may be a time when the physician is seen the least. Staff who have been most involved in the treatment of the patient often withdraw, unable to deal with their sense of inadequacy in fighting off the disease. There is anger directed at God and at the living. Special bitterness is felt toward those who want to help but have never experienced the loss of a child. Strength and succor come from unusual sources: hospital housekeepers, a young student nurse, special friends in the community, people who bring something special of themselves. By the time of death, the family has edged toward some point in the spectrum between bitterness and acceptance.

At one time it was believed that family and patient exhibited different coping behaviors. Chaplain Swanson says that he no longer believes this. Coping behaviors grow out of an individual's attitude toward what he is facing, be it his own death or the death of a loved one. Chaplain Swanson identifies four basic attitudes: self-incrimination, resigned acceptance, faith, and openness to growth.

Most frequently seen is the attitude of self-incrimination: "I'm being condemned and punished for something I have done wrong." The patient or the family member believes he is paying now for an indiscretion. He is paying the price for something he did or did not do. The child remembers when he went to the bathroom outside, or broke a window, or lied, or wished his brother dead. The father or the mother recalls and examines every possible detail of his or her own life. Old ghosts and fears are stirred up as perceived indiscretions,

real or imagined, are reviewed. Often the husband and the wife, each alone with his or her pain, does not wish to further upset the other, and so the isolation begins. There may be subconscious blame directed toward the spouse: "You were never as careful about Johnny's health as you should have been." With this added anger comes more guilt and emotional and physical withdrawal from the marriage.

Self-incrimination is the most common response. Seen less frequently by Chaplain Swanson is an attitude of resigned acceptance. This attitude may be adopted before the crisis or days after the crisis. The death is seen as "just one of those things." "His number was up." Death is viewed as part of life. The parents resign themselves to the idea that within their child are the seeds of disease. They rise to the occasion and do what must be done.

The third coping behavior or rationalization is one of faith. It is a stance that truly derives from the classic definition of faith: faith means tension. The parents hold no expectation for the future; in fact, they see the problem as being out of their hands. They let go of the child and trust in some divine order. Not knowing what will happen, or where they will be led, they remain in a state of suspended tension. They are treading water, yet they are living in faith.

Lastly, there is an attitude of growth and maturity. To suffer is to grow, and there are life-enhancing insights that can accompany a death. Families have expressed to Chaplain Swanson their joy in the strengthening of family ties between husband and wife, and between parents and children. They speak of a refining process through which communication is experienced for the first time. Heart strings unweave. In such a family there are changes in the attitude of the adolescent patient as he nears death. Very young children become mature.

None of these attitudes is better than another, and no individual adopts one stance exclusively. These are coping mechanisms to manage the grief and somehow order the chaos.

Teacher's role with parents in crisis

As a teacher, you might be able to help the parents ease their pain in the loss of their child, for your career is one that joins professional competence with human concern.

As a member of a helping profession, you can perform few more valuable services than to listen. Listening is a basis on which most therapies rest.

There is great need for the family to tell its story often. Repeating the story is one way a family can grasp the reality. A caregiver can listen if the person wants to talk and be a human presence if he does not. In listening one allows others to unlock their feelings and articulate their fears. Listening is particularly helpful during the period of diagnosis, the tortuous period of uncertainty.

A helping person might be able to facilitate communication between the dying child and his family, between the husband and the wife, and between siblings and parents. The objective is to maintain that family unit: the dying child is part of his family as long as he is alive.

The parents should be encouraged not to protect and isolate siblings from the dying child. Siblings need specific facts and information about the disease and the death to allay their own fears. One should be alert to signals suggesting that a sibling is blaming himself. If possible, the brothers and sisters should visit the sick child and touch and play with him, or help care for him if he's at home.

It is important to remember that people do not live constantly at the center of their pain. One day the family will share their pain and frustration, and the next day the family will behave as if the conversation never occurred. The child may feel better, and the situation may appear normal again. But things can change overnight.

A caregiver should not visit a family suffering a crisis with any assumptions about how they are feeling about it. There are many ways to grieve. One does not go wearing a mantle of pity, for pity is dehumanizing and implicit in that stance is a requirement that the one pitied reassure the other. To be an object of pity is an added burden on the ill and on their families.

There are certain phrases to which people resort when visiting someone who is dying or when visiting the family of

someone who is dying. Here are several phrases to avoid:

"It's going to be all right; I just know!" There is no way for anyone to know that. There is always hope, but this type of statement does not deal with the reality of the situation and, in effect, cuts off communication. In addition, the family and the patient feel that they are disappointing the person who makes such a statement when everything worsens. What this visitor is really saying is, "Tell me only the cheerful stuff. I can't deal with the rest."

"I know how you feel." How could anyone possibly know how it feels to be faced with the prospective loss of someone he loves? Even those who have been recently bereaved do not know specifically how that other person feels.

"Let me know if there is anything I can do." How many times we have all said that! Here one is requiring some sort of positive action on the part of those who are already heavy with decisions they cannot make. Better to notice what needs to be done and do it. Bring food, invite the other children to accompany you to the movies, appear with groceries, or run errands.

One's presence is the most eloquent expression of care. Be there! But arrive with some handicraft, or letter-writing or reading material. The family should not have to entertain the visitor. Keep your word! If you say that you will stop by tomorrow at four o'clock or come by next week on Thursday, make certain you do just that. The family must not be let down.

After the funeral, do not disappear! As a caregiver and friend, you are concerned with the integration of the survivors. There may be terrible anger directed toward God, toward the living, toward those who have never experienced the loss of a child. Talk about the child who has died; he must not be killed in the memory of the living.

Make a note of the date a person died and remember the anniversaries: one month after, six months after, one year after. These are very difficult dates. You might write a note, make a phone call, arrange a visit on those days.

As a teacher, it might be unusual to be as directly involved with a family as suggested here. But, surely, in some way you will have an opportunity to support the family or the child. A teacher can be instrumental in the reconciliation of those who are left.

Teacher with child in crisis

As a teacher and friend of a young child in the hospital, your role in the life of that child is dramatic, for in your hands is the ability to lift his spirit. How wonderful for that child to feel that his teacher cares! In showing your concern you are revealing yourself as a friend; you are saying to that child that you will stick by him through his illness and that you hope you will become increasingly meaningful to each other. You have the privilege of being needed, really needed, by another human being. You also have the responsibility of preparing for this need.

The first step of preparation is to ask yourself whether you are really ready that day, right then, to visit a critically ill child. If your own problems are weighing heavily, perhaps you should wait. To enter the world of crisis, you must be able to lay aside your frustrations; you must "shake the dust from your feet."

Examine what you know about the situation. What are the details of Johnny's condition? What course is his illness or condition expected to take? Certainly much of this information could come from his parents. And before any visit, you should call them. You might say to them: "I'd like to visit Johnny. I just wanted to know whether that's all right. Is there anything I should know before I see him? How are things going with you?"

If you get parental approval for your visit, the next step is to call the physician's office. The physician might welcome the opportunity to share his deep concern over the child's deteriorating condition. The physician is doing everything he can to stop the onslaught of disease and is intensely concerned. Identify yourself as the teacher (school nurse, counselor, administrator) and tell the doctor or the nurse that you are going to see Johnny and want to know whether there is anything you should know to make the visit as helpful as possible. He may share something extremely important with you: "Johnny is having difficulty dealing with all the nee-

dles. Maybe you could talk to him about that." Or "He just received some upsetting information this morning."

When you arrive at the hospital, always stop at the nursing station. Every visit should begin there. The nurse can tell you whether it is a poor time to visit, or whether the child is scheduled for tests, or whether the child is heavily medicated. Don't forget that everyone, even the doctor, is working for the head nurse. She is primary in importance in the critical care of that child. When you reach the child's room, knock on his door. If possible, knock twice. This gives the child time to pull his covers up or straighten his bedclothes. Don't just walk into that room: be invited.

When you enter the room, stand by the door. Give the child time to adjust to the fact that someone is there. This is particularly important if the child has been medicated. Never forget that the hospital room is his turf, his terrain. It is his entire world, and you are intruding in his personal space. Let him adjust to you there. Approach the bed slowly. Touch his bed before you touch him. Let him offer you his hand or his arms for a hug. Move slowly.

Depending on his strength, the child in that bed will be the child you knew in the classroom, only exaggerated. A quiet child becomes silent, a noisy child aggressive. The behavior might be strange or different. The child is in crisis, and we must accept him as he is.

Don't assume anything about what Johnny knows or is experiencing. Ask him why he is there or what's happening to him. See what he perceives his situation to be. If he seems fearful, don't say, "I just know you'll be better." Ask him whether he's afraid. If he says yes, get him to be specific. Lurking in the back of his mind, be he four years old or fourteen, are questions about dying: Will it hurt? Where will I go? What really is it? Though some questions can be answered factually, some are in realms of the unknown. If he asks a question you cannot answer, turn it around and ask him what he thinks the answer is. And remember you have no right to contradict what a parent may have said.

A child may wish to remain silent on the whole matter of disease or death. That is his right. But there are little deaths, or traumas, a sick child faces each day. There is the pain of treatment. There are the many needles experienced each day. There are fancy machines and mention of electrodes and electrolytes. "Electricity! Mommy said never to play with electricity!"

There is the painful chest-clapping procedure for children with cystic fibrosis and the antitoxin medication used for leukemia patients that makes them feel worse than when they are not under treatment. There are dye injections; no amount of information on homonyms eases the mind of a five-, six-, or seven-year-old when he hears the word "dye."

There is terrible separation anxiety, especially for the preschool child. Every time Mother leaves, he feels abandoned. In the light of this fear, it is particularly important for you to keep your word. If you say that you will call, or visit, and then do not, you have added to the child's sense of abandonment.

There is great concern over the physical changes caused by the disease or the medication. Hair falls out, limbs swell, faces puff. The responses of the body become unreliable. There are fears of sexual mutilation. The child has watched television and knows from such television shows as "Emergency" and "Marcus Welby, M.D." that mistakes are made, life-threatening errors occur. The awe inspired by fancy machines when viewed from the safety of the family room turns to terror and panic when the child, and not the actor, is hooked to these machines.

There is confusion and terror at the realization that the child's parents cannot protect him from the disease and the pain. There is fear on the part of the child that he may have done some terrible thing—lied, wished a parent dead, played with matches—and is now dying as a result. There is desire to escape the body that is failing him.

Although all these fears and concerns may be swirling around his head, the child may not wish to discuss them. Communication need not be verbal, and you need to be sensitive to many clues. Perhaps the young primary-school child would like to play. You can thumb wrestle with him or bounce a light balloon back and forth. You might

read to the child or have him read to you. Bring books! You know better than anyone what he likes to read. Bring letters from his classmates. Give him a simple assignment in his favorite subject and tell him it needs to be done by next Thursday, when you will return to pick it up. And you had better return next Thursday. Make him a booklet, with questions and graphs and records to be filled out, on the special procedures and treatments he experiences every day in the hospital.

Understand that when the seven-year-old says he feels like a bag of bones he isn't asking you to say, "You're going to be just fine," or, "You look good to me." He may not be fine, and he may, indeed, look awful. The child may really feel like a "bag of bones." He may be dehydrated; he may be thin and perhaps can see his bones; he feels pushed and prodded; perhaps he is so weak that he lies on the bed like a marionette flopped in the corner. Listen to his metaphoric language.

Bring some type of handiwork, be it sewing or papers to correct so that you can sit with the child if he is too weak to talk or not interested in talking.

Remember that as a teacher you have a special place. You represent the child's normal world; you are an oasis for him. The doctors and the nurses bring shots and machines; the parents hover with tears and anguish. You, however, know that child's work-a-day world. You are part of his business and social community. You, more than many, can maintain a semblance of his former world by your visits, news of the classroom, and occasional work assignments. Your interaction with a dying child can keep him among the living a little longer.

Teacher in the classroom

The death of a child in your class, or the death of a child's sibling, is certain to elicit questions from the classmates. But telling the children Anne is in heaven now, and let's get back to work, is no better than telling those children to hide their heads in the sand. Great and terrible questions and fantasies will fill the void if death is not discussed.

Do not pretend to be impassive about a classmate's death. Share with the children your reactions to the sad news. Let the children tell their stories about how they heard, or when they first found out, that there was a problem. Encourage the children to talk about the child and to share stories about the special times they had with that child. "You were his best friend, Brian. What made Johnny so special to you?" Or, "Carol, you took a picture of Johnny last fall when you brought in your camera. Why not bring the photo now?" Let the children write their feelings about that child. The children in that class will need to talk about that death many times. Do not shut off discussion.

Make certain that the children in your class know the details of that child's illness. You need to separate the illness of the child who dies from any medical problems his classmates experience. Stress how unusual the situation was. Emphasize that hospitals are places where people usually get better. The children will have questions about the death itself. Be sensitive to clues that suggest what a child is really trying to find out. The child will want to know whether dying hurt Johnny, whether it is like going to sleep, where he actually is now, and what happened to his body. The child is also wondering, "Will I die soon, too? Will I hurt?" There will be great fascination with the mechanical aspects of death—details of embalming, cremation, and burial. These questions are natural. Seek the answers. Do not suggest that these interests are improper. If you cannot answer a question, turn it around. Ask the child what he thinks. To a child who asks about heaven, say, "Well, what do you think it will be like?" Conflicting religious philosophies may be expressed. Emphasize that people interpret life and death differently. Encourage the children to talk to their families about their classmate's death.

Do not say that Johnny simply went to sleep. You will create a classroom of insomniacs! You will also create great anxiety in those who go to hospitals for tonsillectomies or other routine operations. All children know anesthetics are to put one to sleep!

Nor should you say that God has chosen Johnny to live with him. The children will wonder when God will want another

child to go live with him. The classmates, particularly the siblings, need to be reassured that in no way are they responsible for that child's death. A child who disliked the child who died may feel guilty about his negative feelings; a sister or a brother who before a sudden unexpected death screamed, "I wish you were dead," may need counseling to help relieve the guilt.

If in your classroom you have a sibling of a child who died, you can expect unusual behavior. He may talk about the death constantly, or he may be silent and totally embarrassed by the surrounding attention. This is particularly true if he is in junior high school, where a child wants to be like everyone else. A child whose brother or sister died may experience a terrible slump in his performance, or he may work harder than ever before, as if by being perfect he places himself squarely among the living. The child may feel unloved. Perhaps he should have been the one to die, not his brother! He may interpret the attention and the grief that is focused on the deceased as evidence that the child who died was better loved.

Be aware of the resources in your community. Know where you could direct a family that is having difficulty in coping with the death of a child. As the teacher, you are in a unique position to observe how a child and his family are adjusting to great loss. With the family in turmoil and friends in kindness avoiding the topic of the deceased, you, as the classroom teacher, may well be the one to whom the sibling turns. You may be the one to whom many turn—parents, dying child, and classmates.

Mrs. Russell had opportunities to make a dramatic difference in the lives of those involved with Anne and John, but she was unable to help. She might have helped communication in John's family. In the classroom, she could have helped the children express their questions and fears surrounding Anne's death. There could have been time for shared concern and affection for John and his family. Had she been Anne's teacher, she might have been a special friend and source of strength. These were opportunities lost, opportunities to be meaningful in another's life.

When a Student Dies . . . _____Frances Scott

While walking my dogs early one morning before going to school, I glanced through the newspaper. It was not typical of me to look at the obituary page, but in the brief article listing the most recent deaths was a familiar name. One of my eighth-grade students had died the afternoon before in a house fire.

Standing in the driveway, I wondered how I would manage my feelings that day at school. The tragedy of the loss of a child's life is great. Doctors are prepared in their training for the loss of a patient; clergy are instructed in how to deal with death. But at no time in a teacher's training is a student's death considered.

Soon after arriving at school, I realized that the students were just as shocked and confused as I was. Groups of silent mourners and clusters of students whispering a mix of fact and rumor lined the halls of the junior high school. Homeroom began with the principal's announcement of Melissa's death and a moment of silence. Many students, hearing the news for the first time, rushed sobbing to the restrooms. Others pointed out Melissa's desk to the curious. Students wrestled with their own feelings, anxious for a reaction from their teacher.

My class of thirteen-year-old students seemed to welcome guidance from their English teacher. Many were experiencing death for the first time. Taking my cues from their behavior, I felt that they wanted to talk. Melissa had been shy, and her few close friends voiced their feelings of disbelief. They were watched curiously by other members of the class and given great respect. Others told how they had heard the news and what details they had learned of the fire and the family's sudden move to a neighbor's home.

To channel their feelings, I suggested that we write letters to Melissa's parents, and I quickly reviewed guidelines for writing sympathy notes. The students seemed to welcome the opportunity to organize their thoughts. Discussing plans for their letters with each other appeared to bring relief. Automatically the students made rough drafts, consulted dictionaries, and critiqued each other's notes.

By the next day, many students in the class had visited the family at the funeral parlor and wanted to share the experience. Even though their parents had prepared them for seeing the body, they were still surprised by how strange Melissa looked with makeup and how strong the flowers smelled. During class, the students finished their sympathy notes which I agreed to deliver that evening when I visited the family.

The day of the funeral, Melissa's friends came to school in suits and Sunday dresses. In class they related how their parents had prepared them for what they might see at the church service. They were serious in their grief and anxious to experience this part of life in an adult fashion. By this time, however, Melissa's small circle of friends had greatly broadened. The death of this shy girl had so impressed the student body that few students were left in the eighth-grade classes by the afternoon of the funeral. The day after, students expressed disgust for those who claimed to be close friends of Melissa but attended the funeral merely out of curiosity. Most junior high teachers would not be surprised by this behavior, and they might not even be surprised by the next event.

Later that day the members of the student council announced a collection for the local fire department in Melissa's memory. Since we had not sent flowers, I passed an envelope around the classroom for donations. Commotion erupted, however. I soon learned that one boy who had cried two days before, claiming Melissa was his best friend, had just stolen a dollar from the memorial collection. Some students shouted threats at the boy; others voiced their anger and disgust. Ironically only a day after a funeral, mourners wanted to kill a classmate. The guilty student was put in in-school suspension, more for his own protection than punishment, until the threats and anger diminished.

Every year there have been situations that I have somehow stumbled through, further illustrating the impossibility of training anyone completely for teaching junior high. Melissa's death reminded me of the loss of one of my own classmates and friends, an experience I remember clearly even today. As an adolescent, I was sad and curious about death, funerals, and tragic accidents. As an adult, I knew that my students' experience would stay with them for many years. Mixed with my own feelings of sadness for Melissa's death was an urge to involve myself with my students' confusion and fears. My students turned for comfort to each other, their parents, and their teacher. Sharing experiences during a tragedy develops close personal ties never possible from a traditional curriculum.

Even though my students wanted to talk about the experience, not all groups will respond this way. My sister, also an English teacher, met a different reaction when the student government president at her school died suddenly in a hit-and-run accident. My sister's seniors did not seek involvement with their teachers. They wanted, instead, understanding for their reactions and time to adjust to the tragedy. While writing suggestions for teachers in this situation, one student advised, "Don't pretend nothing's happened. If somebody wants to talk about it, allow it. And please listen to what they have to say."

Besides actively listening, what else could a teacher do to manage the situation? When Melissa died, I learned that English is not something to study but something to practice. Because of the nature of the course, English class can be a positive part of a tragic situation. Teachers should not force a "regular day" upon grieving students. They should, instead, offer choices of activities—outlets for friends, distractions for others. Letters, journals, discussions, and even literature become natural activities, not lessons.

Journal writing especially gives students an emotional outlet, providing an opportunity for them to express their thoughts. Mourners will be dealing with much shock and confusion when they lose a friend. Another of my sister's seniors wrote the following about her journal when the student government president died: "I could hardly write fast enough to get out my confusion, sadness, shock, and a great deal of anger. All the words I wanted to yell and scream I scratched and scribbled until I calmed down and made peace with myself and the situation."

Teachers also can use journals to deal constructively with their own feelings. If the death is a suicide or the result of an accident at school, teachers may have to cope with enormous guilt, doubt, and depression, as well as possible legal problems. Whether writing with students or in private, a teacher can find emotional relief in the activity.

In addition, journals can provide a vehicle for discussing incidents that anger or disgust students. For example, a student's death is an unusual time for everyone in either a junior or senior high school. A sector of the student body will not know genuine compassion for those grieving, and teachers will be watched for behavior to model. Teachers or students could claim close attachment to the victim for the sake of their own reputations; however, close friends generally detect an exaggerated response and do not appreciate a pretentious emotional display. These feelings can be effectively dealt with in journal writing.

Teachers cannot be expected to solve the personal crises students will be experiencing, but they should give some support and understanding. Perhaps one senior best expressed the frustration of dealing with the situation at school when he wrote, "I didn't like it when teachers ignored what had happened and didn't say anything or do anything differently. I didn't like it when teachers gave extra busy work to keep our minds off what had happened. I didn't like it when one teacher let us do nothing at all. I didn't like anything anybody did that day."

Besides attempting activities to help a class in shock, a teacher must attend to certain clerical matters quickly. Students do not like to explain unpleasant situations to substitutes. While changing rolls, teachers should remember to change emergency lesson rolls and seating charts that may have been filed earlier in the year. Also, a computer may require several reminders to "withdraw" a name.

When clearing the student's locker, also clean out files and old sets of papers. Check the bulletin board for work samples. Students do not need unnecessary reminders of the tragedy in the classroom, and the family may want the child's belongings and papers. In fact, a journal entry about death, written by my sister's student a few days before he died, was found by his father and read at his funeral.

A teacher should expect depression in students for weeks after a funeral and may see their grades drop as a result. Teachers should change long-range plans to lighter topics, giving mourners time to adjust emotionally to personal matters and to return to more important topics when they can better concentrate on school. During this period, suggestions for lightening the depression could come from the class members through letters, journal entries, or notes to the teacher. The students may want to rearrange desks or dedicate a publication to their former classmate. While studying literature that involves death or tragic accidents, students may prefer to write their thoughts rather than discuss them in class.

A student's death affects both students and teachers. Work will change, but it will not stop. English class can become a positive part of the tragic experience if a teacher is willing to use the activities and curriculum in a sensitive manner. ■

The Year We Had Aaron

MOLLY OAKLEY

As a teacher, my reaction to "mainstreaming" is one of pure panic. My pulse quickens when I hear the word and I am reminded that mandatory mainstreaming is going to mean new problems for my class and me, problems I can anticipate but cannot even identify. How can I possibly care for and teach those children who need special and individual treatment? How can I presume to teach as well as those with specialized training and diagnostic skills?

When my panic subsides I remind myself mainstreaming is not new to my classroom. I have had an experience that has taught me a lot about "fear" and "difference" and "effects on other children." I realize now that perhaps the experience was not as excruciating or even as threatening as I had feared, but it was frightening, the worry of it was constant, and it was grimly positive. It was a totally human and special experience, and no one in my second grade class that year will ever be the same because of it.

Aaron entered my class on the first day of school in September. Though he was new in our district, I already knew quite a lot about him. From his folder and notes from his parents I had learned that Aaron had bone cancer, that he was undergoing radiation treatment, and that his prognosis was poor. It was feared that he would live only another six to ten months.

I recognized Aaron the minute he walked in. His eyes which were alert and wide looked even bigger because he had no hair. But his smile was friendly, if a little rebellious. His physique was strong though lean for a second-grader.

When I saw that the children were afraid of him I realized that helping Aaron included helping the children understand and accept him. Shortly after the term began, during one of Aaron's absences that were to become more frequent, we had our first discussion. I told the class we had to talk about somebody important to all of us, Aaron. "Why is he bald?" was the first question. "Why is he absent so much?" "Why doesn't he have to take gym?" "Why can't he play with us out on the playground?" Their questions showed that there was already a feeling that Aaron was different.

I explained that he had an illness that tired him easily, that the medicine he took was making his hair fall out. I continued: "How would you like starting a new school feeling strange, with no hair, knowing you looked peculiar?" "How would you feel trying to make new friends and feeling tired and ill at the same time?" I didn't go lightly with them. I was hard on them, not chastizing but really letting them feel for fifteen minutes Aaron's skin and tears and loneliness.

Right away, the next day in fact, the classroom was more relaxed and the children at once began to defend Aaron to the other children in the school lunch line, at the bus stop, and on the playground. They were not going to tolerate others' acting as they had been acting, afraid of a difference.

The first few months Aaron did well in school. He enjoyed reading and searched the library shelves for dinosaur books. He loved looking after our new cage of mice, and for Christmas he made the class a huge "pin-the-tail-on-the-mouse" game. He was alert and seemed strong with a strength that could easily be translated into stubbornness, even an arrogance that shrieked independence.

Shortly after Christmas Aaron started getting weaker and had to cut down school to half a day, alternating mornings and afternoons. More frequently now I had to talk to the class. I gathered them all on the rug in our small library section. Huddled close together, we talked about how to help Aaron more. I reminded them how hard it must be to be ill for so long.

After a time he was almost never able to come to school. At one of our library corner discussions we decided to buy Aaron a gerbil cage to house two mice from our rapidly growing family. We selected four children from the class to accompany me in a visit to Aaron with the cage, two mice, and a fifty-pound bag of wood shavings. He was delighted with his gift. The visit was such a success that we began going weekly. Each Thursday four children, a different quartet each time, crowded into my dilapidated VW with presents, letters and more wood shavings for the mouse cage. Though Aaron was not in class each day, he was still one of us. We would not let his absence exclude him from our activities.

Aaron came back to class once more. That day he was suffering, and he could not help complaining about pain in his back. His parents and I had decided he should try to endure this two-hour rescheduling. We tried to make him as comfortable as possible with sleeping mats piled for support on his chair. He sat through math and an art project, and he must have been in agony, for only two days later we learned that the cancer had spread to his back and that his spinal cord had disintegrated in that area, the cause of his severe pain that day.

The announcement a day or two later that Aaron was in the hospital was accepted by the class in sober silence. Huddled again in our library ring, we talked in a new way about Aaron's illness. Till that time I had never mentioned cancer, for as long as Aaron himself was unaware of the nature of his illness, I felt it would be unfair to divulge this to the class. But after conferring with his parents, I told the children that Aaron had cancer.

The ability of these second-graders to understand astounded me. I should have known that cancer was no stranger to some who had had relatives who died of it or were suffering from it now; I should have remembered they learned more from television than we adults liked to admit.

But I did not get the full impact of their maturity until Margaret asked: "What are his chances?" My answer, "Not good." Margaret persisted. "I don't mean that. What are the percentages that he'll not live?" In my surprise I blurted out, "Ninety to ninety-five." Margaret got her answer, and she burst into tears.

The class was stunned by this new dimension to our problem, for now they did not perceive this as Aaron's problem or even his parents' problem but a part of their own family hurting and suffering. When Aaron's mother called me a week later I was overjoyed for I had not expected to see Aaron again. Not only was Aaron better, he was home from the hospital. Would I like to talk to him? What a wonderful moment, to hear his happy voice on the telephone!

Aaron did not come to school again. We made one more visit, then no more because the excitement of seeing his classmates tired him. May and June were long months. The joy of spring and the marvel at what had been accomplished as a class that year were contrasted with our concern and worry for one of us. We continued sending a stream of letters, drawings, little books and puzzles. Whenever one of us felt the need, we had one of our intimate library talks. The children tried to understand how the suffering felt and why it could not be stopped. As a teacher, I was trying to prepare them for Aaron's death. While we talked about hope and strength, we did discuss death, and it was understood that Aaron might die soon.

While my principal knew and approved of the direction I had taken in preparing the children for the probability of Aaron's death, several teachers were disapproving. I should not be making such a big deal, they said. But I could not imagine ever ignoring my second-graders' thirst for answers and understanding. I could never insult their keenness and openness by playing with their love of a friend or their fear for him. They had to discover and fulfill their need to grieve.

On the last day of school, June 22, 1977, we gathered on the library rug. I told the children that Aaron had died that morning. We cried together. Then I answered questions. It was important to the children that he had died at home and not at the hospital. Despite their sophistication in knowing about cancer, they were young children after all. They asked many questions about how Aaron felt when he died, how his parents felt. Did Aaron have his teddy bear with him? Did it go with him? Was he in pain now?

In our class book we wrote the last entry, "Aaron died today. We loved him very much," and we pasted in a picture of him taken at our fun-filled silly Halloween party so long ago.

The bell rang. I handed out the report cards. Then the children left, and I left, scattering to the summer, never to come together again to huddle in the library corner. We took our grief for Aaron with us.

Appendices

Appendix A
Materials for Children and Young Adults:
A List

FICTION

Aaron, Chester. *Catch Calico!* New York: E. P. Dutton, 1979. Intermediate/Middle.

Abbot, Sarah. *The Old Dog*. New York: Coward, McCann & Geoghegan, Inc., 1972. Intermediate.

Agee, James. *A Death in the Family*. New York: McDowell, Obolensky, 1957. High.

Alcott, Louisa May. *Little Women*. Boston: Little, Brown & Co., 1968. Intermediate/Middle.

Alexander, Sue. *Nadia the Willful*. New York: Pantheon Books, Inc., 1983. Primary.

Aliki. *The Two of Them*. New York: Greenwillow Books, 1979. Preschool/Primary.

Alter, Judy. *After Pa Was Shot*. New York: William Morrow & Co., Inc., 1978. Intermediate/Middle.

Althea. *When Uncle Bob Died*. Great Britain: Dinosaur Publications, 1982. Intermediate.

Angell, Judie. *Ronnie and Rosey*. Scarsdale, NY: Bradbury Press, 1977. Intermediate/Middle.

Annixter, Paul. *Swiftwater*. New York: Hill & Wang, Inc., 1950. Middle/High.

Armstrong, William. *Sounder*. New York: Harper & Row Publishers, Inc., 1969. Intermediate.

———. *Sourland*. New York: Harper & Row Publishers, Inc., 1971. Intermediate/Middle.

Arundel, Honor. *The Blanket Word*. Nashville, TN: Thomas Nelson, Inc., 1973. Middle/High.

Asher, Sandy. *Missing Pieces*. New York: Delacorte Press, 1984. Middle/High.

Babbitt, Natalie. *The Eyes of the Amaryllis*. New York: Farrar, Straus & Giroux, Inc., 1977. Intermediate/Middle.

Baird, Thomas. *Walk Out a Brother*. New York: Harper & Row Publishers, Inc., 1983. Middle/High.

Balderson, Margaret. *When Jays Fly to Barbmo*. Cleveland, OH: William Collins Publishers, Inc., 1969. Middle.

Barford, Carol. *Let Me Hear the Music*. Boston: Houghton Mifflin Co., 1979. Intermediate/Middle.

Bartoli, Jennifer. *Nonna*. New York: Harvey House Publishers, 1975. Primary.

Bauer, Marion Dane. *Shelter from the Wind*. New York: Seabury Press, Inc., 1976. Intermediate/Middle.

Bawden, Nina. *Squib*. Philadelphia, PA: J. B. Lippincott Co., 1971. Intermediate/Middle.

Beckman, Gunnel. *Admission to the Feast*. New York: Holt, Rinehart & Winston, Inc., 1972. Middle.

———. *That Early Spring*. New York: The Viking Press, Inc., 1975. Middle.

Beim, Jerrold. *With Dad Alone*. New York: Harcourt Brace Jovanovich, Inc., 1954. Preschool/Primary.

Benchley, Nathaniel. *A Necessary End: A Novel of World War II*. New York: Harper & Row Publishers, Inc., 1976. Middle.

Bloch, Marie Halun. *Displaced Person*. New York: Lothrop, Lee & Shepard Co., 1978. Intermediate/Middle.

Blue, Rose. *Grandma Didn't Wave Back*. New York: Franklin Watts, Inc., 1972. Primary/Intermediate.

———. *Nikki 108*. New York: Franklin Watts, Inc., 1973. Intermediate/Middle.

———. *The Thirteenth Year: A Bar Mitzvah Story*. New York: Franklin Watts, Inc., 1977. Intermediate/Middle.

Blume, Judy. *Tiger Eyes*. Scarsdale, NY: Bradbury Press, 1981. Intermediate/Middle.

Bond, Nancy. *A Place To Come Back To*. New York: Atheneum Publishers, 1984. Intermediate/Middle.

———. *A String in the Harp*. New York: Atheneum Publishers, 1976. Intermediate/Middle.

Borack, Barbara. *Someone Small*. New York: Harper & Row Publishers, Inc., 1969. Primary.

Bosse, Malcolm J. *Cave beyond Time*. New York: Thomas Y. Crowell Co., 1980. Intermediate/Middle.

Bradbury, Bianca. *"I'm Vinny, I'm Me."* Boston: Houghton Mifflin Co., 1977. Intermediate/Middle.

————. *Where's Jim Now?* Boston: Houghton Mifflin Co., 1978. Intermediate/Middle.

Brancato, Robin F. *Facing Up*. New York: Alfred A. Knopf, Inc., 1984. Middle/High.

Brenner, Barbara. *A Year in the Life of Rosie Bernard*. New York: Avon Books, 1983. Intermediate/Middle.

Bridgers, Sue Ellen. *Home before Dark*. New York: Alfred A. Knopf, Inc., 1976. Middle/High.

Bro, Margueritte Harmon. *Sarah*. Garden City, NY: Doubleday & Co., Inc., 1949. Middle.

Brooks, Jerome. *Uncle Mike's Boy*. New York: Harper & Row Publishers, Inc., 1973. Intermediate/Middle.

Brown, Margaret Wise. *The Dead Bird*. Reading, MA: Addison-Wesley Publishing Co., Inc., 1965. Preschool/Primary.

Brown, Roy. *Find Debbie!* Boston: Houghton Mifflin Co., 1976. Intermediate/Middle.

Buck, Pearl S. *The Beech Tree*. Binghamton, NY: John Day Company, Inc., 1955. Primary/Intermediate.

————. *The Big Wave*. New York: Scholastic Book Services, 1960. Intermediate.

Bulla, Clyde. *The Beast of Lor*. New York: Thomas Y. Crowell Co., 1977. Intermediate/Middle.

Bunting, Eve. *The Empty Window*. New York: Frederick Warne & Co., Inc., 1980. Intermediate.

————. *The Happy Funeral*. New York: Harper & Row Publishers, Inc., 1982. Preschool/Primary.

Burch, Robert Joseph. *Simon and the Game of Chance*. New York: The Viking Press, Inc., 1970. Intermediate/Middle.

Burchard, P. *Bimby*. New York: Coward, McCann & Geoghegan, Inc., 1968. Primary/Intermediate.

Byars, Betsy. *Goodbye, Chicken Little*. New York: Harper & Row Publishers, Inc., 1979. Intermediate/Middle.

————. *The Two-Thousand-Pound Goldfish*. New York: Harper & Row Publishers, Inc., 1982. Intermediate.

Callen, Larry. *The Deadly Mandrake*. Boston: Little, Brown & Co., 1978. Intermediate/Middle.

Cameron, Eleanor. *Beyond Silence*. New York: E. P. Dutton, 1980. Middle.

————. *That Julia Redfern*. New York: E. P. Dutton, 1982. Primary/Intermediate.

Campbell, R. Wright. *Where Pigeons Go to Die*. New York: Rawson Associates Publishers, Inc., 1978. Middle.

Carmer, Chas. *Tawny*. New York: Macmillan Publishing Co., Inc., 1978. Intermediate/Middle.

Carpenter, W. S. and Bluenose, P. *Two Knots on a Counting Rope*. New York: Holt, Rinehart & Winston, Inc., 1964. Primary/Intermediate.

Carrick, Carol. *The Accident*. Boston: Houghton Mifflin Co., 1976. Primary.

Cate, Dick. *Never Is a Long, Long Time*. Nashville, TN: Thomas Nelson, Inc., 1976. Intermediate.

Chambers, Aidan. *Dance on My Grave*. New York: Harper & Row Publishers, Inc., 1983. High.

Cleaver, Vera and Cleaver, Bill. *Grover*. Philadelphia, PA: J. B. Lippincott Co., 1970. Intermediate.

————. *A Little Destiny*. New York: Lothrop, Lee & Shepard Books, 1979. Intermediate/Middle.

————. *Where the Lilies Bloom*. Philadelphia, PA: J. B. Lippincott Co., 1969. Intermediate/Middle.

Clifford, Eth. The Killer Swan. Boston: Houghton Mifflin Co., 1980. Intermediate/Middle.

Clifton, Lucille. *Everett Anderson's Goodbye*. New York: Holt, Rinehart & Winston, Inc., 1983. Preschool/Primary.

Coburn, John B. *Anne and the Sand Dobbies: A Story of Death for Children and Their Parents*. New York: Seabury Press, Inc., 1964. Intermediate.

Coerr, Eleanor B. *Sadako and the Thousand Paper Cranes*. New York: Putnam Publishing Group, 1977. Primary/Intermediate.

Cohen, Barbara. *Thank You, Jackie Robinson*. New York: Lothrop, Lee & Shepard Books, 1974. Intermediate/Middle.

Coleman, Hila. *Sometimes I Don't Love My Mother*. New York: William Morrow & Co., Inc., 1977. Middle.

Collier, James and Collier, Christopher. *The Bloody Country*. New York: Four Winds Press, 1977. Middle.

————. *My Brother Sam Is Dead*. New York: Four Winds Press, 1974. Middle.

Cooney, Barbara. *The Courtship, Merry Marriage, and Feast of Cock Robin and Jenny Wren, to Which is Added the Doleful Death of Cock Robin*. New York: Charles Scribner's Sons, 1965. Preschool/Primary.

Cormier, Robert. *The Bumblebee Flies Anyway*. New York: Pantheon Books, Inc., 1983. Middle/High.

————. *The Chocolate War*. New York: Pantheon Books, Inc., 1974. Middle.

————. *I Am the Cheese*. New York: Pantheon Books, Inc., 1977. Middle/High.

Coutant, Helen. *First Snow*. New York: Alfred A. Knopf, Inc., 1974. Primary.

Craven, Margaret. *I Heard the Owl Call My Name*. Garden City, NY: Doubleday & Co., Inc., 1973. High.

Crawford, Charles P. *Three-Legged Race*. New York: Harper & Row Publishers, Inc., 1974. Middle/High.

Cresswell, Helen. *Dear Shrink*. New York: Macmillan Publishing Co., Inc., 1982. Middle.

Crutcher, Chris. *Running Loose*. New York: Greenwillow Books, 1983. Middle/High.

Cunningham, Julia. *Burnish Me Bright*. New York: Pantheon Books, Inc., 1970. Intermediate.

———. *Tuppenny*. New York: E. P. Dutton, 1978. Intermediate/Middle.

———. *Wings of the Morning*. Los Angeles: Golden Gate Junior Books, 1971. Primary.

DeBruyn, Monica. *The Beaver Who Wouldn't Die*. Chicago: Follett Publishing Company, 1975. Primary/Intermediate.

Degens, T. *Transport 7-41-R*. New York: The Viking Press, Inc., 1974. Middle.

De Paola, Tomie. *Nana Upstairs & Nana Downstairs*. New York: G. P. Putnam's Sons, 1973. Preschool/Primary.

Derman, Martha. *Friendstone*. New York: The Dial Press, 1981. Intermediate/Middle.

Dexter, Pat Egan. *The Emancipation of Joe Tepper*. Nashville, TN: Thomas Nelson, Inc., 1976. Middle/High.

Distad, Audree. *The Dream Runner*. New York: Harper & Row Publishers, Inc., 1977. Intermediate/Middle.

Dixon, Paige. *May I Cross Your Golden River*. New York: Atheneum Publishers, 1975. Middle.

———. *Skipper*. New York: Atheneum Publishers, 1979. High.

———. *A Time to Love—A Time to Mourn* (originally published as *May I Cross Your Golden River*). New York: Scholastic Book Services, 1975. Middle.

Dobrin, Arnold. *Scat!* New York: Four Winds Press, 1971. Primary.

Donavan, John. *Wild in the World*. New York: Harper & Row Publishers, Inc., 1971. Intermediate/Middle.

Donnelly, Elfie. *So Long Grandpa*. New York: Crown Publishers, Inc., 1981. Intermediate.

Duncombe, Frances. *Summer of the Burning*. New York: Putnam Publishing Group, 1976. Intermediate/Middle.

Estes, Winston. *Another Part of the House*. Philadelphia, PA: J. B. Lippincott Co., 1970. Middle.

———. *Homefront*. Philadelphia, PA: J. B. Lippincott Co., 1976. High.

Farley, Carol J. *The Garden Is Doing Fine*. New York: Atheneum Publishers, 1975. Intermediate/Middle.

Fassler, Joan. *My Grandpa Died Today*. New York: Behavioral Publications, Inc., 1971. Primary.

Feagles, Anita MacRae. *The Year the Dreams Came Back*. New York: Atheneum Publishers, 1976. Intermediate/Middle.

Fisher, Leonard Everett. *The Death of Evening Star: The Diary of a Young New England Whaler*. Garden City, NY: Doubleday & Co., Inc., 1972. Intermediate/Middle.

Fitzhugh, Louise and Scoppettone, Sandra. *Bang Bang You're Dead*. New York: Harper & Row Publishers, Inc., 1969. Preschool/Primary.

Fontane, Theodor. *Sir Ribbeck of Ribbeck of Havelland*. New York: Macmillan Publishing Co., Inc., 1968. Preschool/Primary.

Forman, James D. *The Pumpkin Shell*. New York: Farrar, Straus & Giroux, Inc., 1981. High.

French, Michael. *Pursuit*. New York: Delacorte Press, 1982. Middle/High.

Gardam, Jane. *The Summer after the Funeral*. New York: Macmillan Publishing Co., Inc., 1973. Middle/High.

Garden, Nancy. *Loners*. New York: The Viking Press, Inc., 1972. Middle.

Gelman, Rita and Friedman, Warner. *Uncle Hugh: A Fishing Story*. New York: Harcourt Brace Jovanovich, Inc., 1978. Preschool/Primary.

George, John and George, Jean. *Vulpes, The Red Fox*. New York: E. P. Dutton, 1948. Intermediate.

Gipson, Fred. *Old Yeller*. New York: Harper & Row Publishers, Inc., 1965. Intermediate/Middle.

Girion, Barbara. *Tangle of Roots*. New York: Charles Scribner's Sons, 1979. Middle.

Glaser, Diane. *The Diary of Trilby Frost*. New York: Holiday House, Inc., 1976. Intermediate/Middle.

Graeber, Charlotte. *Mustard*. New York: Macmillan Publishing Co., Inc., 1982. Primary/Intermediate.

Green, Constance C. *Beat the Turtle Drum*. New York: The Viking Press, Inc., 1976. Intermediate/Middle.

Green, Phyllis. *Empty Seat*. New York: Elsevier/Nelson Publishing Co., 1980. Intermediate/Middle.

———. *New Mother for Martha*. New York: Human Sciences Press, 1978. Preschool/Primary.

Greenberg, Jan. *A Season In-Between*. New York: Farrar, Straus & Giroux, Inc., 1979. Intermediate/Middle.

Greenfield, Eloise. *Sister*. New York: Thomas Y. Crowell Co., 1974. Intermediate.

Grimes, Nikki. *Growin'*. New York: The Dial Press, 1977. Primary/Intermediate.

Guest, Judith. *Ordinary People*. New York: The Viking Press, Inc., 1976. High.

Guy, Rosa. *The Friends*. New York: Holt, Rinehart & Winston, Inc., 1973. Middle.

Hall, Lynn. *Flowers of Anger*. Chicago: Follett Publishing Co., 1976. Middle.

———. *Shadows*. Chicago: Follett Publishing Co., 1977. Intermediate.

———. *Sticks and Stones*. Chicago: Follett Publishing Co., 1972. Middle/High.

Harnden, Ruth Peabody. *The High Pasture*. Boston: Houghton Mifflin Co., 1964. Intermediate.

Hartling, Peter. *Oma*. New York: Harper & Row Publishers, Inc., 1977. Primary/Intermediate.

Hegwood, Mamie. *My Friend Fish*. New York: Holt, Rinehart & Winston, Inc., 1975. Primary.

Hellberg, Hans-Eric. *Ben's Lucky Hat*. New York: Crown Publishers, Inc., 1982. Intermediate.

Hermes, Patricia. *Nobody's Fault?* New York: Harcourt Brace Jovanovich, Inc., 1981. Intermediate/Middle.

———. *Who Will Take Care of Me?* New York: Harcourt Brace Jovanovich, Inc., 1983. Intermediate.

———. *You Shouldn't Have to Say Good-bye*. New York: Harcourt Brace Jovanovich, Inc., 1982. Middle/High.

Hinton, S. E. *The Outsiders*. New York: The Viking Press, Inc., 1967. Middle.

———. *That Was Then, This Is Now*. New York: The Viking Press, Inc., 1971. Middle.

Holland, Isabelle. *Alan and the Animal Kingdom*. Philadelphia, PA: J. B. Lippincott Co., 1977. Intermediate/Middle.

———. *The Man without a Face*. Philadelphia, PA: J. B. Lippincott Co., 1972. Middle.

———. *Of Love and Death and Other Journeys*. Philadelphia, PA: J. B. Lippincott Co., 1975. Middle/High.

Hoopes, Lyn Littlefield. *Nana*. New York: Harper & Row Publishers, Inc., 1981. Preschool/Primary.

Howe, Norma. *God, the Universe, and Hot Fudge Sundaes*. Boston: Houghton Mifflin Co., 1984. Middle/High.

Hughes, Monica. *Hunter in the Dark*. New York: Atheneum Publishers, 1983. Intermediate/Middle.

Hunt, Irene. *Across Five Aprils*. Chicago: Follett Publishing Co., 1964. Intermediate/Middle.

———. *The Lottery Rose*. New York: Charles Scribner's Sons, 1976. Middle/High.

———. *Up a Road Slowly*. Chicago: Follett Publishing Co., 1966. Middle.

———. *William*. New York: Charles Scribner's Sons, 1977. Intermediate/Middle.

Hunter, Mollie. *A Sound of Chariots*. New York: Harper & Row Publishers, Inc., 1972. Middle.

———. *The Stronghold*. New York: Harper & Row Publishers, Inc., 1974. Middle/High.

———. *The Third Eye*. New York: Harper & Row Publishers, Inc., 1979. Middle/High.

Huntsberry, William E. *The Big Hang-Up*. New York: Lothrop, Lee & Shepard Books, 1970. Middle/High.

Hurd, Edith Thacher. *Black Dog Who Went into the Woods*. New York: Harper & Row Publishers, Inc., 1980. Preschool/Primary.

Ish-Koshor, Sulamith. *Our Eddie*. New York: Pantheon Books, Inc., 1969. Middle.

Jansson, Tove. *The Summer Book*. New York: Pantheon Books, Inc., 1975. Intermediate/Middle.

Jones, Penelope. *Holding Together*. Scarsdale, NY: Bradbury Press, 1981. Intermediate.

Kantrowitz, Mildred. *When Violet Died*. New York: Parents' Magazine Press, 1973. Primary.

Kaplan, Bess. *The Empty Chair*. New York: Harper & Row Publishers, Inc., 1978. Intermediate/Middle.

Kennedy, Richard. *Come Again in the Spring*. New York: Harper & Row Publishers, Inc., 1976. Intermediate.

Kerr, Judith. *The Other Way Round*. New York: Coward, McCann & Geoghegan, Inc., 1975. Intermediate/Middle.

———. *A Small Person Far Away*. New York: Coward, McCann & Geoghegan, Inc., 1979. Intermediate/Middle.

———. *When Hitler Stole Pink Rabbit*. New York: Coward, McCann & Geoghegan, Inc., 1972. Intermediate/Middle.

Kidd, Ronald. *That's What Friends Are For*. Nashville, TN: Thomas Nelson, Inc., 1978. Intermediate/Middle.

Kingman, Lee. *Break a Leg, Betsy Maybe!* Boston: Houghton Mifflin Co., 1976. Middle.

Klein, Norma. *Confessions of an Only Child*. New York: Pantheon Books, Inc., 1974. Intermediate/Middle.

Korschunow, Irina. *Who Killed Christopher?* New York: Putnam Publishing Group, 1980. Middle/High.

Kuskin, Karla. *The Bear Who Saw the Spring*. New York: Harper & Row Publishers, Inc., 1961. Primary/Intermediate.

Lamorisse, Albert. *The Red Balloon*. Garden City, NY: Doubleday & Co., Inc., 1956. Primary/Intermediate.

Lawrence, Louise. *Sing and Scatter Daisies*. New York: Harper & Row Publishers, Inc., 1977. Middle.

Lawson, Robert. *Rabbit Hill*. New York: The Viking Press, Inc., 1944. Intermediate.

Lee, Mildred S. *Fog*. New York: Seabury Press, Inc., 1972. Intermediate/Middle.

———. *The Skating Rink*. New York: Seabury Press, Inc., 1969. Intermediate.

Lee, Virginia. *The Magic Moth*. New York: Seabury Press, Inc., 1972. Intermediate.

L'Engle, Madeleine. *Meet the Austins*. New York: Vanguard Press, Inc., 1960. Intermediate/Middle.

———. *A Ring of Endless Light*. New York: Farrar, Straus & Giroux, Inc., 1980. Intermediate/Middle.

Levit, Rose. *Ellen: A Short Life Long Remembered*. New York: Bantam Books, 1974. Middle/High.

Lichtman, Wendy. *Blew and the Death of the Mag*. Monroe, UT: Freestone Publishing Co., 1975. Intermediate/Middle.

Lindgren, Astrid. *Brothers Lionheart*. New York: The Viking Press, Inc., 1975. Intermediate/Middle.

Little, Jean. *Home from Far*. Boston: Little, Brown & Co., 1965. Intermediate/Middle.

Lorenzo, Carol Lee. *Heart-of-Snowbird*. New York: Harper & Row Publishers, Inc., 1975. Middle/High.

———. *Mama's Ghosts*. New York: Harper & Row Publishers, Inc., 1974. Intermediate/Middle.

Love, Sandra. *Dive for the Sun*. Boston: Houghton Mifflin Co., 1982. Middle.

Lowry, Lois. *Autumn Street*. Boston: Houghton Mifflin Co., 1980. Intermediate/Middle.

———. *A Summer to Die*. Boston: Houghton Mifflin Co., 1977. Intermediate.

Lutters, Valerie A. *The Haunting of Julie Unger*. New York: Atheneum Publishers, 1977. Intermediate.

McCaffrey, Anne. *Dragonsong*. New York: Atheneum Publishers, 1976. Intermediate/Middle.

Maclachlan, Patricia. *Cassie Binegar*. New York: Harper & Row Publishers, Inc., 1982. Intermediate/Middle.

McLendon, Gloria. *My Brother Joey Died*. New York: Julian Messner, 1982. Intermediate.

Madison, Winifred. *A Portrait of Myself*. New York: Random House, Inc., 1979. Middle/High.

Mann, Peggy. *There Are Two Kinds of Terrible*. Garden City, NY: Doubleday & Co., Inc., 1977. Intermediate.

Marshall, James Vance. *Walkabout*. New York: William Morrow & Co., Inc., 1971. Middle.

Mathis, Sharon. *Listen for the Fig Tree*. New York: The Viking Press, Inc., 1974. Middle.

———. *Teacup Full of Roses*. New York: The Viking Press, Inc., 1972. Middle.

Mazer, Norma Fox. *A Figure of Speech*. New York: Delacorte Press, 1973. Intermediate/Middle.

———. *When We First Met*. New York: Four Winds Press, 1983. Middle/High.

Miles, Betty. *The Trouble with Thirteen*. New York: Alfred A. Knopf, Inc., 1979. Intermediate.

Miles, Miska. *Annie and the Old One*. Boston: Little, Brown & Co., 1971. Primary/Intermediate.

Mills, Claudia. *All the Living*. New York: Macmillan Publishing Co., Inc., 1983. Intermediate.

Moe, Barbara A. *Pickles and Prunes*. New York: McGraw-Hill Publications Co., 1976. Intermediate/Middle.

Mohr, Nicholasa. *El Bronx Remembered*. New York: Harper & Row Publishers, Inc., 1975. Middle/High.

———. *Nilda*. New York: Harper & Row Publishers, Inc., 1973. Intermediate/Middle.

Molloy, Anne Stearns. *The Girl from Two Miles High*. New York: Hastings-House Publishers, Inc., 1967. Intermediate.

Moody, Anne. *Mr. Death: Four Stories*. New York: Harper & Row Publishers, Inc., 1975. Intermediate/Middle.

Naylor, Phyllis Reynolds. *Night Cry*. New York: Atheneum Publishers, 1984. Intermediate/Middle.

———. *A String of Chances*. New York: Atheneum Publishers, 1982. Middle.

———. *To Walk the Sky Path*. Chicago: Follett Publishing Co., 1973. Intermediate/Middle.

Ness, Evaline. *Sam, Bangs, and Moonshine*. New York: Holt, Rinehart & Winston, Inc., 1966. Preschool/Primary.

Norman, Lilith. *Climb a Lonely Hill*. New York: Henry Z. Walck, Inc., 1972. Middle.

Norris, Gunilla Brodde. *The Friendship Hedge*. New York: E. P. Dutton, 1973. Primary/Intermediate.

O'Dell, Scott. *Child of Fire*. Boston: Houghton Mifflin Co., 1974. Middle.

———. *Island of the Blue Dolphins*. Boston: Houghton Mifflin Co., 1960. Intermediate/Middle.

———. *Zia*. Boston: Houghton Mifflin Co., 1976. Intermediate/Middle.

Oneal, Zibby. *A Formal Feeling*. New York: The Viking Press, Inc., 1982. Middle/High.

Orgel, Doris. *The Mulberry Music*. New York: Harper & Row Publishers, Inc., 1971. Intermediate.

Osborne, Mary Pope. *Run Run, As Fast As You Can*. New York: The Dial Press, 1982. Middle.

Paterson, Katherine. *Bridge to Terabithia*. New York: Thomas Y. Crowell Co., 1977. Intermediate/Middle.

Paulsen, Gary. *The Foxman*. Nashville, TN: Thomas Nelson, Inc., 1977. Middle.

———. *Tracker*. Scarsdale, NY: Bradbury Press, 1984. Intermediate/Middle.

Peavy, Linda S. *Allison's Grandfather*. New York: Charles Scribner's Sons, 1981. Primary/Intermediate.

Peck, Richard. *Close Enough to Touch*. New York: Delacorte Press, 1981. Middle/High.

———. *Dreamland Lake*. New York: Holt, Rinehart & Winston, Inc., 1973. Middle.

———. *Father Figure*. New York: The Viking Press, Inc., 1978. Middle.

Peck, Robert Newton. *A Day No Pigs Would Die*. New York: Alfred A. Knopf, Inc., 1972. Middle.

Pevsner, Stella. *And You Give Me A Pain, Elaine*. New York: Seabury Press, Inc., 1978. Middle.

Pfeffer, Susan Beth. *About David*. New York: Delacorte Press, 1980. Middle/High.

Phipson, Joan. *A Tide Flowing*. New York: Atheneum Publishers, 1981. Intermediate/Middle.

Platt, Kin. *Hey, Dummy*. Philadelphia, PA: Chilton Book Co., 1971. Middle.

Pollowitz, Melinda. *Cinnamon Cane*. New York: Harper & Row Publishers, Inc., 1977. Intermediate/Middle.

Rabe, Bernice. *The Girl Who Had No Name*. New York: E. P. Dutton, 1977. Intermediate/Middle.

———. *Naomi*. Nashville, TN: Thomas Nelson, Inc., 1975. Intermediate/Middle.

Rabin, Gil. *Changes*. New York: Harper & Row Publishers, Inc., 1973. Intermediate/Middle.

Rawlings, Marjorie K. *The Yearling*. New York: Grosset & Dunlap, 1938. Intermediate/Middle.

Rees, David. *Risks*. Nashville, TN: Thomas Nelson, Inc., 1977. Intermediate/Middle.

Rhodin, Eric. *The Good Greenwood*. Philadelphia, PA: Westminster Press, 1971. Intermediate.

Rinaldi, Ann. *Term Paper*. New York: Walker & Co., 1980. High.

Rinaldo, C. L. *Dark Dreams*. New York: Harper & Row Publishers, Inc., 1974. Middle.

Roberts, Jane. *Emir's Education in the Proper Use of Magical Powers*. New York: Delacorte Press, 1979. Intermediate.

Rock, Gail. *The House without a Christmas Tree*. New York: Alfred A. Knopf, Inc., 1974. Primary/Intermediate.

———. *The Thanksgiving Treasure*. New York: Alfred A. Knopf, Inc., 1974. Primary/Intermediate.

Rushing, Jane Gilmore. *Mary Dove: A Love Story*. Garden City, NY: Doubleday & Co., Inc., 1974. Middle/High.

———. *Winds of Blame*. Garden City, NY: Doubleday & Co., Inc., 1983. Middle/High.

Sachs, Marilyn. *Beach Towels*. New York: E. P. Dutton, 1982. Intermediate/Middle.

Salten, Felix. *Bambi*. New York: Simon & Schuster, Inc., 1929. Intermediate.

Samuels, Gertrude. *Run, Shelly, Run!* New York: Thomas Y. Crowell Co., 1974. Middle.

Schoen, Barbara. *A Place and a Time*. New York: Thomas Y. Crowell Co., 1967. Middle/High.

Schotter, Roni. *A Matter of Time*. Cleveland, OH: William Collins Publishers, Inc., 1979. Middle.

Scoppettone, Sandra. *Trying Hard to Hear You*. New York: Harper & Row Publishers, Inc., 1974. Middle/High.

Sherburne, Zoa. *Girl in the Mirror*. New York: William Morrow & Co., Inc., 1966. Intermediate/Middle.

Shotwell, Louisa R. *Adam Bookout*. New York: The Viking Press, Inc., 1967. Intermediate.

Shreve, Susan Richards. *Family Secrets: Five Very Important Stories*. New York: Alfred A. Knopf, Inc., 1979. Primary/Intermediate.

Simon, Norma. *We Remember Philip*. Chicago: Albert Whitman & Co., 1979. Primary/Intermediate.

Slepian, Jan. *Lester's Turn*. New York: Macmillan Publishing Co., Inc., 1981. Intermediate/Middle.

Slote, Alfred. *Hang Tough, Paul Mather*. Philadelphia, PA: J. B. Lippincott Co., 1973. Intermediate.

Smith, Doris B. *A Taste of Blackberries*. New York: Thomas Y. Crowell Co., 1973. Intermediate.

Smith, Robert Kimmel. *The War with Grandpa*. New York: Delacorte Press, 1984. Intermediate/Middle.

Speare, Elizabeth George. *The Bronze Bow*. Boston: Houghton Mifflin Co., 1961. Intermediate/Middle.

Sperry, Armstrong. *Call It Courage*. New York: Macmillan Publishing Co., 1940. Intermediate/Middle.

Stanek, Muriel. *I Won't Go without a Father*. Chicago: Albert Whitman, 1972. Primary.

Stevens, Carla. *Stories from a Snowy Meadow*. New York: Seabury Press, Inc., 1976. Primary.

Stevens, Margaret. *When Grandpa Died*. Chicago: Children's Press, 1979. Preschool/Primary.

Stolz, Mary. *By the Highway Home*. New York: Harper & Row Publishers, Inc., 1971. Middle.

———. *The Edge of Next Year*. New York: Harper & Row Publishers, Inc., 1974. Intermediate/Middle.

Strasser, Tod. *Friends 'Til the End*. New York: Delacorte Press, 1981. Middle/High.

Strete, Craig. *When Grandfather Journeys into Winter*. New York: Greenwillow Books, 1979. Intermediate.

Stretton, Barbara. *You Never Lose*. New York: Alfred A. Knopf, Inc., 1982. Middle/High.

Stull, Edith G. *My Turtle Died Today*. New York: Holt, Rinehart & Winston, Inc., 1964. Primary.

Talbot, Toby. *Away Is So Far*. New York: Four Winds Press, 1974. Primary/Intermediate.

———. *Dear Greta Garbo*. New York: Putnam Publishing Group, 1978. Intermediate/Middle.

Tarlton, Gillian Leigh. *The Two Worlds of Coral Harper*. New York: Harcourt Brace Jovanovich, Inc., 1983. Intermediate/Middle.

Taylor, Mildred. *Roll of Thunder Hear My Cry*. New York: The Dial Press, 1976. Intermediate/Middle.

Taylor, Theodore. *Teetoncey*. Garden City, NY: Doubleday & Co., Inc., 1974. Intermediate/Middle.

Thiele, Colin. *Fire in the Stone*. New York: Harper & Row Publishers, Inc., 1974. Middle/High.

———. *Storm Boy*. New York: Harper & Row Publishers, Inc., 1978. Intermediate.

Thomas, Ianthe. *Hi, Mrs. Mallory!* New York: Harper & Row Publishers, Inc., 1979. Preschool/Primary.

Thomas, Joyce Carol. *Bright Shadow*. New York: Avon Books, 1983. Middle.

Tobias, Tobi. *Petey*. New York: Putnam Publishing Group, 1978. Primary.

Tolan, Stephanie S. *Grandpa—And Me*. New York: Charles Scribner's Sons, 1978. Intermediate/ Middle.

Townsend, Maryann and Stern, Ronnie. *Pop's Secret*. Reading, MA: Addison-Wesley Publishing Co., 1980. Primary/Intermediate.

Uchida, Yoshiko. *The Birthday Visitor*. New York: Charles Scribner's Sons, 1975. Primary.

Varley, Susan. *Badger's Parting Gift*. New York: Lothrop, Lee & Shepard Books, 1984. Intermediate/ Middle.

Viorst, Judith. *The Tenth Good Thing about Barney*. New York: Atheneum Publishers, 1971. Preschool/ Primary.

Vogel, Ilse-Margret. *My Twin Sister Erika*. New York: Harper & Row Publishers, Inc., 1976. Primary/ Intermediate.

Voight, Cynthia. *Dicey's Song*. New York: Atheneum Publishers, 1982. Intermediate/Middle.

Walker, Mary Alexander. *Year of the Cafeteria*. Indianapolis, IN: Bobbs-Merrill Co., Inc., 1971. Middle.

Walsh, Jill Paton. *Unleaving*. New York: Farrar, Straus & Giroux, Inc., 1976. Middle.

Warburg, Sandol S. *Growing Time*. Boston: Houghton Mifflin Co., 1969. Preschool/Primary.

Wersba, Barbara. *The Dream Watcher*. New York: Atheneum Publishers, 1968. Middle.

———. *Run Softly, Go Fast*. New York: Atheneum Publishers, 1972. Middle/High.

White, E. B. *Charlotte's Web*. New York: Harper & Row Publishers, Inc., 1952. Primary/Intermediate.

White, Paul. *What's Happened to Aunt Jean?* London: Scripture Union, 1976. Intermediate.

Whitehead, Ruth. *The Mother Tree*. New York: Seabury Press, Inc., 1971. Primary/Intermediate.

Wiggin, Kate Douglas. *The Bird's Christmas Carol*. Boston: Houghton Mifflin Co., 1941. Intermediate.

Wilkinson, Brenda. *Ludell and Willie*. New York: Harper & Row Publishers, Inc., 1977. Middle.

Windsor, Patricia. *The Summer Before*. New York: Harper & Row Publishers, Inc., 1973. Middle.

Winthrop, Elizabeth. *Walking Away*. New York: Harper & Row Publishers, Inc., 1973. Intermediate/ Middle.

Wojciechowska, Maia. *Don't Play Dead before You Have To*. New York: Harper & Row Publishers, Inc., 1970. Middle.

Woodford, Peggy. *Please Don't Go*. New York: E. P. Dutton, 1973. Intermediate/Middle.

Woods, George A. *Catch a Killer*. New York: Harper & Row Publishers, Inc., 1972. Middle/High.

Yep, Laurence. *Liar, Liar*. New York: William Morrow & Co., 1983. Middle/High.

York, Carol Beach. *Remember Me When I Am Dead*. New York: Elsevier/Nelson Publishing Co., Inc., 1980. Intermediate.

Zalben, Jane Breskin. *Maybe It Will Rain Tomorrow*. New York: Farrar, Straus & Giroux, Inc., 1982. Middle.

Zindel, Bonnie and Zindel, Paul. *A Star for the Latecomer*. New York: Harper & Row Publishers, Inc., 1980. Middle.

Zindel, Paul. *Pardon Me You're Stepping on My Eyeball*. New York: Harper & Row Publishers, Inc., 1976. Intermediate.

———. *The Pigman*. New York: Harper & Row Publishers, Inc., 1968. Middle.

Zolotow, Charlotte. *A Father Like That*. New York: Harper & Row Publishers, Inc., 1971. Preschool/ Primary.

———. *My Grandson Lew*. New York: Harper & Row Publishers, Inc., 1974. Preschool/Primary.

NONFICTION

Adler, Charles S., et al., eds. *We Are But a Moment's Sunlight: Understanding Death*. New York: Pocket Books, Inc., 1976. Middle/High.

Anders, Rebecca. *A Look at Death*. Minneapolis, MN: Lerner Publications Co., 1978. Primary/Intermediate.

Anderson, Lydia. *Death*. New York: Franklin Watts, Inc., 1980. Intermediate.

Anonymous. *Go Ask Alice*. Englewood Cliffs, NJ: Prentice-Hall, Inc., 1971. High.

Aries, Philippe. *Western Attitudes toward Death*. Baltimore, MD: Johns Hopkins University Press, 1974. High.

Arnothy, Christine. *I Am Fifteen—And I Don't Want to Die*. New York: E. P. Dutton, 1956. Middle.

Asinof, Eliot. *Craig and Joan: Two Lives for Peace*. New York: The Viking Press, Inc., 1971. Middle/ High.

Barnard, Christiaan. *Good Life Good Death: A Doctor's Case for Euthanasia and Suicide*. Englewood Cliffs, NJ: Prentice-Hall, Inc., 1980. High.

Bernstein, Joanne E. *Books to Help Children Cope with Separation and Loss*. 2d ed. New York: Bowker, 1983. High/Adult.

———. *Loss and How to Cope with It*. New York: Seabury Press, Inc., 1977. Middle/High.

Bernstein, Joanna E. and Gullo, Steven. *When People Die*. New York: E. P. Dutton, 1977. Preschool/Primary.

Bradley, Buff. *Endings: A Book about Death*. Reading, MA: Addison-Wesley Publishing Co., Inc., 1979. Intermediate/Middle/High.

Butler, Robert N. *Why Survive? Being Old in America*. New York: Harper & Row Publishers, Inc., 1975. High/Adult.

Coffin, Margaret. *Death in Early America*. New York: Elsevier/Nelson Publishing Co., Inc., 1976. Middle/High.

Corley, Elizabeth A. *Tell Me about Death: Tell Me about Funerals*. Santa Clara, CA: Grammatical Sciences, 1973. Intermediate.

Feifel, Herman, ed. *New Meanings of Death*. New York: McGraw-Hill Publications Co., 1977. High/Adult.

Friedman, Marcia. *Story of Josh*. New York: Praeger Publishers, Inc., 1974. High/Adult.

Fulton, Robert and Bendikser, Robert, eds. *Death and Identity*. 2d ed. Bowie, MD: Charles Press Publishers, Inc., 1976. High/Adult.

Grollman, Earl A. *Living When a Loved One Has Died*. Boston: Beacon Press, 1977. High/Adult.

————. *Talking about Death: A Dialogue between Parent and Child*. Boston: Beacon Press, 1976. Preschool/Primary.

Gunther, John. *Death Be Not Proud: A Memoir*. New York: Harper & Row Publishers, Inc., 1949. High/Adult.

Hamilton-Paterson, James and Andrews, C. *Mummies: Death and Life in Ancient Egypt*. New York: The Viking Press, Inc., 1979. Middle/High.

Harris, Audrey Jane. *Why Did He Die?* Minneapolis, MN: Lerner Publications Company, 1965. Primary/Intermediate.

Henry, Marguerite. *A Pictorial Life Story of Misty*. Chicago: Rand McNally & Co., 1976. Middle.

Hughes, Phyllis R. *Dying Is Different*. Mahomet, IL: Mech Mentor Educational Publishers, 1978. High/Adult.

Hürlimann, Bettina. *Barry: The Story of a Brave St. Bernard*. New York: Harcourt Brace Jovanovich, Inc., 1968. Primary/Intermediate.

Hyde, Margaret O. and Forsyth, Elizabeth Held. *Suicide: The Hidden Epidemic*. New York: Franklin Watts, Inc., 1978. Middle/High.

Jones, Mary Alice. *Tell Me about Heaven*. Chicago: Rand McNally & Co., 1956. Preschool/Primary.

Kastenbaum, Robert. *Death, Society, & Human Experience*. 2d ed. Saint Louis, MO: The C. V. Mosby Co., 1981. High/Adult.

Klagsburn, Francine. *Too Young to Die: Youth and Suicide*. Boston: Houghton Mifflin Co., 1976. Middle/High.

Klein, Norma. *Sunshine*. New York: Holt, Rinehart & Winston, Inc., 1975. Middle/High.

Klein, Stanley. *The Final Mystery*. Garden City, NY: Doubleday & Co., Inc., 1974. Intermediate.

Krementz, Jill. *How It Feels When a Parent Dies*. New York: Alfred A. Knopf, Inc., 1981. Intermediate/Middle.

Kübler-Ross, Elisabeth. *Living with Death and Dying*. New York: Macmillan Publishing Co., Inc., 1981. High.

————. *On Death and Dying*. New York: Macmillan Publishing Co., Inc., 1969. High/Adult.

————. *Questions and Answers on Death and Dying*. New York: Macmillan Publishing Co., Inc., 1974. High/Adult.

————. *To Live Until We Say Good-Bye*. Englewood Cliffs, NJ: Prentice-Hall, Inc., 1978. Middle/High.

Landau, Elaine. *Death: Everyone's Heritage*. New York: Julian Messner, 1976. Intermediate.

Langone, John. *Death Is a Noun: A View of the End of Life*. Boston: Little, Brown & Co., 1972. High.

————. *Vital Signs: The Way We Die in America*. Boston: Little, Brown & Co., 1974. High.

L'Engle, Madeleine. *The Summer of the Great Grandmother*. New York: Farrar, Straus & Giroux, Inc., 1974. High/Adult.

LeShan, Eda. *Learning to Say Good-Bye: When a Parent Dies*. New York: Macmillan Publishing Co., Inc., 1976. Intermediate/Middle.

Lifton, Robert Jay and Olson, Eric. *Living and Dying*. New York: Praeger Publishers, Inc., 1974. High/Adult.

Lund, Doris. *Eric*. Philadelphia, PA: J. B. Lippincott Co., 1974. Middle/High.

McHugh, Mary. *Young People Talk about Death*. New York: Franklin Watts, Inc., 1980. Middle.

Madison, Arnold. *Suicide and Young People*. Boston: Houghton Mifflin Co., 1978. Intermediate/Middle.

Mayle, Peter. *"Will I Go to Heaven?"* New York: Corwin Books, 1976. Primary/Intermediate.

Mendoza, George. *The Hunter I Might Have Been*. New York: Astor-Honor, Inc., 1968. Intermediate.

Mills, Gretchen C., et al. *Discussing Death: A Guide to Death Education*. Palm Springs, CA: ETC Publications, 1976. High/Adult.

Moody, Raymond A., Jr. *Life after Life*. St. Simons Island, GA: Mockingbird Books, 1975. High/Adult.

Morgan, Ernest. *A Manual of Death Education & Simple Burial*. 9th ed. Burnsville, NC: Celo Press, 1980. High/Adult.

Morris, Jeannie. *Brian Piccolo: A Short Season*. New York: Dell Publishing Co., Inc., 1972. Middle/High.

Pringle, Laurence. *Death Is Natural*. New York: Four Winds Press, 1977. Intermediate/Middle.

Quinlan, Joseph and Quinlan, Julia. *Karen Ann: The Quinlans Tell Their Story*. Garden City, NY: Doubleday & Co., 1977. High/Adult.

Raab, Robert A. *Coping with Death*. Rev. ed. New York: Rosen Publishing Group, 1982. High.

Rabkin, Brenda. *Growing Up Dead: A Hard Look at Why Adolescents Commit Suicide*. Nashville, TN: Abingdon Press, 1979. High/Adult.

Read, Piers Paul. *Alive: The Story of the Andes Survivors*. Philadelphia, PA: J. B. Lippincott Co., 1974. High.

Russell, Olive Ruth. *Freedom to Die: Moral and Legal Aspects of Euthanasia*. New York: Dell Publishing Co., Inc., 1976. High/Adult.

Sanderlin, Johnny. *Johnny*. Cranbury, NJ: A. S. Barnes & Co., Inc., 1968. Middle/High.

Segerberg, Osborn. *Living with Death*. New York: E. P. Dutton, 1976. Intermediate.

Shneidman, Edwin, ed. *Suicidology: Contemporary Developments*. New York: Grune & Stratton, 1976. High/Adult.

Shoenberg, Bernard, et al., eds. *Anticipatory Grief*. New York: Columbia University Press, 1974. High/Adult.

Simon, Seymour. *Life and Death in Nature*. New York: McGraw-Hill Publications Co., 1976. Intermediate.

Stanford, Gene and Perry, Deborah. *Death Out of the Closet: A Curriculum Guide to Living with Dying*. New York: Bantam Books, 1976. High/Adult.

Stein, Sara Bonnett. *About Dying: An Open Family Book for Parents and Children Together*. New York: Walker & Co., 1974. Primary.

Tresselt, Alvin R. *The Dead Tree*. New York: Parents' Magazine Press, 1972. Preschool/Primary.

Turner, Ann Warren. *Houses for the Dead: Burial Customs through the Ages*. New York: David McKay Co., 1976. High/Adult.

Veatch, Robert M. *Death, Dying, and the Biological Revolution*. New Haven, CT: Yale University Press, 1976. High.

Watts, Richard G. *Straight Talk about Death with Young People*. Philadelphia, PA: Westminster Press, 1975. Middle/High.

Wilcox, Sandra G. and Sutton, Marilyn. *Understanding Death and Dying*. Sherman Oaks, CA: Alfred Publishing Co., Inc., 1977. High/Adult.

Young, Jim. *When the Whale Came to My Town*. New York: Alfred A. Knopf, Inc., 1974. Intermediate.

Zim, Herbert S. and Bleeker, Sonia. *Life and Death*. New York: William Morrow & Co., Inc., 1970. Intermediate.

AUDIOVISUAL

Across Five Aprils [Filmstrip]. New York: Miller-Brody Productions, Inc., 1974, 2 rolls, col., 1 cassette or phonodisc. Intermediate/Middle.

All Living Things: The Great Cycle of Life and Death [Filmstrip]. Wilton, CT: Current Affairs Films, 1976, 4 rolls, col., 4 cassettes. Primary.

All the Way Home [Motion Picture]. New York: Dynamic Films, Inc., 1958, 16mm, b&w, 30 min. High/Adult.

And We Were Sad, Remember? [Motion Picture]. Washington, DC: U.S. Office of Education, Division of Educational Technology/National Audiovisual Center, Order Section, 1978, 16mm, col., 30 min. High/Adult.

Annie and the Old One [Motion Picture]. Santa Monica, CA: BFA Educational Media, 1976, 16mm, col., 15 min. Primary/Intermediate.

Bridge to Terabithia [Filmstrip]. New York: Random House School Division, 1981, 2 rolls, col., 2 cassettes, teacher's guide. Intermediate.

But He Was Only Seventeen: The Death of a Friend [Filmstrip]. Pleasantville, NY: Sunburst Communications, 1981, 3 rolls, col., 3 cassettes, teacher's guide. Middle/High.

But Jack Was a Good Driver [Motion Picture]. Del Mar, CA: CRM Films, 1974, 16mm, col., 15 min. Middle/High.

Call It Courage [Filmstrip]. Miller-Brody Productions, Inc., 1972, 2 rolls, col., 1 cassette or phonodisc. Intermediate/Middle.

Charlotte's Web [Filmstrip]. Pasadena, CA: Barr Films, 1974, 3 rolls, col., 3 cassettes, teacher's guide. Primary/Intermediate.

Chickamauga [Motion Picture]. New York: Contemporary Films/McGraw-Hill Films, 1968, 16mm, b&w, 33 min. High/Adult.

Children in Crisis: Death [Filmstrip]. Elmsford, NY: Parents' Magazine Films, 1975, 5 rolls, col., 3 cassettes or 1 phonodisc. High.

Cipher in the Snow [Motion Picture]. Burbank, CA: Informational Materials, Inc., 1973, 16mm, col., 24 min. Intermediate/Middle/High.

The Day Grandpa Died [Motion Picture]. Santa Monica, CA: BFA Educational Media, 1970, 16mm, col., 12 min. Intermediate/Middle/High.

The Dead Bird [Filmstrip]. New York: McGraw-Hill, Inc., 1972, 1 roll, col., 1 cassette or phonodisc, teacher's manual. Primary.

Death—A Natural Part of Living [Filmstrip]. Shawnee Mission, KS: Marsh Film Enterprises, 1977, 1 roll, col., 1 cassette or phonodisc. Intermediate/Middle.

Death and Dying: Closing the Circle [Filmstrip]. Mt. Kisco, NY: Guidance Associates, 1975, 5 rolls, col., 5 cassettes or phonodiscs, teacher's guide. Middle/High.

Death Be Not Proud [Filmstrip]. Jamaica, NY: Eye Gate Media, 1978, 1 roll, col., 1 cassette, discussion guide. Middle/High.

Death: Coping with Loss [Motion Picture]. Chicago, IL: Coronet Instructional Media, 1976, 16mm, col., 19 min. High/Adult.

Death: Facing a Loss [Filmstrip]. Chicago, IL: Society for Visual Education, 1978, 4 rolls, col., 4 cassettes or phonodiscs. Intermediate.

Death: How Can You Live with It? [Motion Picture]. Burbank, CA: Walt Disney Educational Media, 1977, 16mm, col., 21 min. Intermediate/Middle/High.

Death in Literature [Filmstrip]. Mt. Kisco, NY: Guidance Associates, [n.d.], 2 rolls, col., 2 cassettes or phonodiscs, teacher's guide. High.

Death of a Gandy Dancer [Motion Picture]. New York: Learning Corporation of America, 1977, 16mm, col., 26 min. Middle/High.

Death—Part of Life [Filmstrip]. Mt. Kisco, NY: Guidance Associates, 1978, 2 rolls, col., 1 cassette or phonodisc. Intermediate.

Depression and Suicide: You Can Turn Bad Feelings into Good Ones [Motion Picture]. Toronto, Canada: Document Associates, Inc., 1976, 16mm, col., 26 min. High/Adult.

A Dignified Exit [Motion Picture]. New York: Filmakers Library, 1981, 16mm, col., 26 min. High/Adult.

Dimensions of Death [Filmstrip]. DeKalb, IL: Educational Perspectives Associates, 1977, 10 rolls, 10 cassettes. High.

Dying [Motion Picture]. Boston: WGBH-TV, Educational Foundation, 1976, 16mm, col., 97 min. Middle/High/Adult.

Echoes [Motion Picture]. Mt. Kisco, New York: Guidance Associates, 1974, 16mm, col., 11 min. Middle/High.

Emily, the Story of a Mouse [Motion Picture]. Briarcliff Manor, NY: Benchmark Films, Inc., 1975, 16mm, col., 5 min. Preschool/Primary.

Extending Life [Motion Picture]. Santa Monica, CA: BFA Educational Media, 1976, 16mm, col., 15 min. Middle/High.

Families in Crisis: Coping with Death [Filmstrip]. Chicago, IL: Coronet Instructional Media, 1976, 1 roll, col., 1 cassette. Intermediate/Middle.

Family Problems: Dealing with Crisis [Filmstrip]. Burbank, CA: Walt Disney Educational Media Company, 1980, 6 rolls, col., 6 cassettes, teacher's guide. Primary/Intermediate.

The Following Sea [Motion Picture]. New York: McGraw-Hill Films, 1971, 16mm, b&w, 11 min. High.

Footsteps on the Ceiling [Motion Picture]. New York: Phoenix Films, 1981, 16mm, col., 8 min. Intermediate/Middle.

The Garden Party [Motion Picture]. Hollywood, CA: Paramount Communications, 1973, 16mm, col., 24 min. High/Adult.

Gramp: A Man Ages and Dies [Filmstrip]. Pound Ridge, NY: Sunburst Communications, Inc., 1976, 1 roll, col., 1 cassette or phonodisc, teacher's guide. Middle/High.

Help Me! The Story of a Teenage Suicide [Videocassette]. Los Angeles: S.L. Film Productions, 1977, 1¾ in. videocassette, col., 25 min. High/Adult.

How Death Came to Earth [Motion Picture]. New York: National Film Board of Canada, 1972, 16mm, col., 14 min. Middle/High/Adult.

I Want to Die [Motion Picture]. Pacific Palisades, CA: Paulist Productions, 1977, 16mm, col., 25 min. High/Adult.

Island of the Blue Dolphins [Filmstrip]. Cambridge, MA: Films, Inc., 1981, 2 rolls, col., 2 cassettes, teacher's guide. Intermediate/Middle.

Jocelyn [Motion Picture]. New York: Filmakers Library, 1980, 16mm, col., 28 min. Middle/High.

Last Rites: A Child's Reaction to Death [Motion Picture]. New York: Filmakers Library, 1978, 16mm, col., 30 min. Middle/High/Adult.

Living with Dying [Filmstrip]. Pound Ridge, NY: Sunburst Communications, Inc., 1973, 2 rolls, col., 2 cassettes or phonodiscs, teacher's guide. Intermediate.

Loss and Grief [Filmstrip]. Costa Mesa, CA: Concept Media, 1977, 7 rolls, col., 7 phonodiscs, instructor's manual. Middle/High.

The Magic Moth [Motion Picture]. Lawrence, KS: Centron Educational Films, 1976, 16mm, col., 22 min. Intermediate/Middle/High.

Marek [Motion Picture]. New York: Time-Life Multimedia, 1978, 16mm, col., 45 min. High/Adult.

A Matter of Time [Motion Picture]. New York: Learning Corporation of America, 1981, 16mm, col., 30 min. Middle/High.

My Brother Sam Is Dead [Filmstrip]. New York: Random House School Division, 1981, 2 rolls, col., 2 cassettes, teacher's guide. Intermediate/Middle.

My Grandson Lew [Motion Picture]. Pasadena, CA: Barr Films, 1976, 16mm, col., 13 min. Primary/Intermediate.

My Turtle Died Today [Motion Picture]. Santa Monica, CA: BFA Educational Media, 1968, 16mm, col., 8 min. Preschool/Primary.

Old Yeller [Filmstrip]. Jamaica, NY: Eye Gate Media, 1978, 1 roll, col., 1 cassette, discussion guide. Intermediate/Middle.

Peacebird [Sound Recording]. Los Angeles: Franciscan Communications, 1974, 33 rpm phonodisc or cassette. Middle/High.

Perspective on Death [Filmstrip]. Pound Ridge, NY: Sunburst Communications, Inc., 1976, 2 rolls, col., 2 cassettes or phonodiscs, teacher's guide. Middle/High.

Perspectives on Death: A Thematic Teaching Unit [Filmstrip]. DeKalb, IL: Educational Perspectives Associates, 1972, 2 rolls, col., 4 cassettes. High.

Poetry of Death [Filmstrip]. Morton, IL: Spectrum Educational Media, 1974, 2 rolls, col., 2 cassettes. High.

Preventing Teen Suicide: You Can Help [Filmstrip]. Pleasantville, NY: Sunburst Communications, 1980, 3 rolls, col., 3 cassettes or phonodiscs, teacher's guide. Middle/High.

Rabbit [Motion Picture]. Evanston, IL: Eccentric Circle Cinema Workshop, 1971, 16mm, col., 15 min. Intermediate/Middle.

Rabbit Hill [Motion Picture]. New York: Contemporary Films/McGraw-Hill, Inc., 1967, 16mm, col., 60 min. Primary/Intermediate.

Richie [Motion Picture]. New York: Learning Corporation of America, 1978, 16mm, col., 31 min. High/Adult.

The Right to Die? [Filmstrip]. Wilton, CT: Current Affairs Films, 1977, 1 roll, col., 1 cassette. Middle/High.

A Ring of Endless Light [Sound Recording]. New York: Miller-Brody Productions, Inc., 1981, cassette. Intermediate/Middle.

Ronnie's Tune [Motion Picture]. Ossining, NY: Wombat Productions, Inc., 1978, 16mm, col., 18 min. Middle/High.

Sandcastle [Filmstrip]. New York: Image Publications, 1971, 1 roll, col., 1 cassette or phonodisc. Intermediate/Middle.

A Shocking Accident [Motion Picture]. Los Angeles: Direct Cinema Ltd., 1982, 16mm, col., 25 min. Middle/High.

Sounder [Filmstrip]. Jamaica, New York: Eye Gate Media, 1978, 1 roll, col., 1 cassette, discussion guide. Intermediate/Middle.

Storm Boy [Motion Picture]. New York: Learning Corporation of America, 1976, 16mm, col., 33 min. Intermediate/Middle.

The Street [Motion Picture]. New York: National Film Board of Canada, 1976, 16mm, col., 10 min. High/Adult.

String Bean [Motion Picture]. New York: Contemporary Films/McGraw-Hill Films, 1964, 16mm, col., 17 min. Intermediate.

Suicide: Who Will Cry for Me? [Filmstrip]. Pleasantville, NY: Audiovisual Narrative Arts, 1979, 3 rolls, col., 3 cassettes. Middle/High.

Talking about Death with Children [Filmstrip]. Batesville, IN: Batesville Management Services, 1980, 1 roll, col., 1 cassette. Intermediate/Middle.

Teenage Suicide [Filmstrip]. Stanford, CA: Multimedia Productions, 1981, 1 roll, col., 1 cassette, teacher's guide. Middle/High.

Themes in Literature: Death [Filmstrip]. Mt. Kisco, NY: Guidance Associates, 1977, 2 rolls, col., 2 cassettes. High.

Things in Their Season [Motion Picture]. New York: Learning Corporation of America, 1975, 16mm, col., 79 min. High/Adult.

This One for Dad [Motion Picture]. Pacific Palisades, CA: Paulist Productions, 1978, 16mm, col., 18 min. Middle/High.

To Be Aware of Death [Motion Picture]. New York: Billy Budd Films, 1974, 16mm, col., 15 min. High/Adult.

Uncle Monty's Gone [Motion Picture]. New York: McGraw-Hill Films, 1976, 16mm, col., 14 min. Primary/Intermediate.

Understanding Changes in the Family: Playing Dead [Filmstrip]. Mt. Kisco, NY: Guidance Associates, 1973, 1 roll, col., 1 cassette or phonodisc. Primary/Intermediate.

Understanding Death: A Basic Program in Death and Dying [Filmstrip]. Jamaica, NY: Eye Gate Media, 1976, 6 rolls, col., 3 cassettes. Middle/High.

Understanding Death Series [Filmstrip]. DeKalb, IL: Educational Perspectives Associates, 1974, 5 rolls, col., 5 cassettes, 5 guides. Intermediate.

Up a Road Slowly [Filmstrip]. New York: Random House School Division, 1980, 2 rolls, col., 2 cassettes. Intermediate/Middle.

Very Good Friends [Motion Picture]. New York: Learning Corporation of America, 1976, 16mm, col., 29 min. Intermediate/High.

What if a Crisis Hits Your Family?: Since Mom Died [Filmstrip]. Jamaica, NY: Eye Gate Media, 1976, 1 roll, col., 1 cassette. Intermediate.

When Disaster Strikes: Coping with Loss, Grief and Rejection [Filmstrip]. Pleasantville, NY: Human Relations Media, 1980, 3 rolls, col., 3 cassettes, teacher's guide. High.

Where Is Dead? [Motion Picture]. Chicago, IL: Encyclopedia Britannica Educational Corporation, 1975, 16mm, col., 19 min. Primary/Intermediate.

Whose Life Is It Anyway? [Motion Picture]. Briarcliff Manor, NY: Benchmark Films, Inc., 1975, 16mm, col., 53 min. High/Adult.

The Yearling [Filmstrip]. Wilmette, IL: Films, Inc., 1975, 3 rolls, b&w, 3 cassettes, teacher's guide. Intermediate/Middle.

You See—I've Had a Life [Motion Picture]. Irvine, CA: Doubleday Multimedia, 1972, 16mm, b&w, 35 min. High/Adult.

The Young Man and Death [Motion Picture]. Mount Vernon, NY: Macmillan Films, 1976, 16mm, col., 16 min. High/Adult.

The Youth Killers [Filmstrip]. Pleasantville, NY: Audiovisual Narrative Arts, 1973, 2 rolls, col., 2 cassettes or phonodiscs. Middle/High.

Appendix B
Organizations and Associations

The following is a highly selective listing of organizations and associations that continue to support the informational needs of children and adults for a variety of subjects relevant to this topic. A brief overview of purpose/goals/objectives with major publications is given for each. Samples of the materials each provides is available free upon request by letter or phone call.

American Association of Suicidology, 2459 S. Ash St., Denver, CO 80222. (303) 692-0985.
Devoted to research and service in the field of suicide prevention, crisis intervention, and life-threatening behaviors. Publications: *Suicide and Life-Threatening Behavior* (quarterly journal), *Newslink* (newsletter). Brochures: "Suicide in Youth and What You Can Do About It—A Guide for Students/A Guide for School Personnel," "Suicide Prevention in the Classroom." Order from North Wales Press, PO Box 1486, North Wales, PA 19454.

Centre for Living with Dying, 2542 S. Bascom Ave., Suite 225, Campbell, CA 95008. (408) 377-8533.
Began in 1976 as a volunteer counseling service for patients and their families facing threatening illness and for those deeply affected by the approaching or actual death of others. Publications: *Centre Outreach* (newsletter), informational brochures and bibliographies for children and adults.

The Compassionate Friends, Inc., P.O. Box 1347, Oak Brook, IL 60521. (312) 323-5010.
This nationwide support group for bereaved parents consists of 383 local volunteer chapters throughout the United States. Addresses for these chapters are available upon request. Brochures: "Understanding Grief," "When a Child Dies," "Stillbirth, Miscarriage and Infant Death," "Caring for Surviving Children," "Suggestions for Teachers and School Counselors," and "Suggestions for Doctors and Nurses." Annotated listing of monographs also available.

Concern for Dying, 250 W. 57th St., New York, NY 10017. (212) 246-6962.
Began in 1967 to protect patient autonomy in regard to treatment during terminal illness and to prevent the futile prolongation of the dying process and needless suffering by the dying. Will provide upon request information about "The Living Will," a document which "enables individuals, while competent, to give their directions for treatment during terminal illness." Publications: *Concern for Dying Newsletter* (quarterly), conference proceedings, legal guide to the Living Will, articles, films. Also provides a speakers bureau on the subject of death and dying.

Foundation of Thanatology, 630 W. 168th St., New York, NY 10032.
Founded in 1967 and based at Columbia Presbyterian Medical Center, this foundation is dedicated to promoting vastly improved psychosocial and medical care for patients who are critically ill or dying from cancer, heart disease, stroke, diabetes, and other diseases and to including their families in this care. Sponsors a series of symposia on issues in health care and provides literature in the form of books, papers, research reports, and monographs.

The Hastings Center, 360 Broadway, Hastings-on-Hudson, NY 10706. (914) 478-0500.
The center was founded in 1969 and its goals are advancement of research on those issues that develop as a response to advances in medicine, the biological sciences, and the social and behavioral sciences; stimulation of universities and professional schools to support the teaching of ethics; and public education. Publications: *The Hastings Center Report, IRB: A Review of Human Subjects Research,* article reprints, and bibliographies.

Leukemia Society of America, 800 Second Ave., New York, NY 10017. (212) 573-8484.
Established in 1949, the society's major purpose is to encourage leukemia research on a worldwide basis. Also provides patient aid for those individuals presently afflicted with the

disease. Publications: annual report. Brochures: "Facts about the Leukemia Society of America, Inc.," "Leukemia," "Emotional Aspects of Childhood Leukemia: A Handbook for Parents."

Make-A-Wish Foundation of America, 4601 N. 16th St., Suite 205, Phoenix, AZ 85016. (602) 234-0960.
An organization for children dying of a terminal illness. It was established to transform a little person's fantasy into an actual experience. Numerous chapters have recently been established throughout the U.S especially in large cities.

Office of Cancer Communications, National Cancer Institute, Building 31, Room 10A18, Bethesda, MD 20205. (301) 496-4000.
Provides pamphlets and brochures for children, parents, and educators on all aspects of cancer treatment and effects. Some publications are available free upon request. Brochures: "Students with Cancer: A Resource for the Educator," "Young People with Cancer: A Handbook for Parents," "Hospital Days-Treatment Ways: Coloring Book."

Appendix C
You & Death: A Questionnaire

This questionnaire was designed by Edwin Shneidman of the Center for Advanced Study in the Behavioral Sciences, in consultation with Edwin Parker and G. Ray Funkhouser of Stanford University. It is a modification of a questionnaire Shneidman developed at Harvard with the help of four graduate assistants: Chris Dowell, Ross Goldstein, Dan Goleman, and Bruce Smith.

    The instrument and/or the individual responses might be useful to motivate discussion among students and adults and encourage these groups to share their reactions, attitudes, questions, and experiences about death. Not all of the 75 questions are appropriate for young children; therefore, the user should be selective in determining questions that are matched with the cognitive and emotional levels of youngsters.

1. Who died in your first personal involvement with death?
   - ☐ A. Grandparent or great-grand-parent.
   - ☐ B. Parent.
   - ☐ C. Brother or sister.
   - ☐ D. Other family member.
   - ☐ E. Friend or acquaintance.
   - ☐ F. Stranger.
   - ☐ G. Public figure.
   - ☐ H. Animal.

2. To the best of your memory, at what age were you first aware of death?
   - ☐ A. Under three.
   - ☐ B. Three to five.
   - ☐ C. Five to 10.
   - ☐ D. Ten or older.

3. When you were a child, how was death talked about in your family?
   - ☐ A. Openly.
   - ☐ B. With some sense of discomfort.
   - ☐ C. Only when necessary and then with an attempt to exclude the children.
   - ☐ D. As though it were a taboo subject.
   - ☐ E. Never recall any discussion.

4. Which of the following best describes your childhood conceptions of death?
   - ☐ A. Heaven-and-hell concept.
   - ☐ B. After-life.
   - ☐ C. Death as sleep.
   - ☐ D. Cessation of all physical and mental activity.
   - ☐ E. Mysterious and unknowable.
   - ☐ F. Something other than the above.
   - ☐ G. No conception.
   - ☐ H. Can't remember.

5. Which of the following most influenced your present attitudes toward death?
   - ☐ A. Death of someone close.
   - ☐ B. Specific reading.
   - ☐ C. Religious upbringing.
   - ☐ D. Introspection and meditation.
   - ☐ E. Ritual (e.g., funerals).
   - ☐ F. TV, radio or motion pictures.
   - ☐ G. Longevity of my family.
   - ☐ H. My health or physical condition.
   - ☐ I. Other (specify): _____

6. Which of the following books or authors have had the most effect on your attitude toward death?
   - ☐ A. The Bible.
   - ☐ B. Camus.
   - ☐ C. Hesse.
   - ☐ D. Agee.
   - ☐ E. Shakespeare.
   - ☐ F. Mann.
   - ☐ G. No books or authors.
   - ☐ H. Other (specify): _____

7. How much of a role has religion played in the development of your attitude toward death?
   - ☐ A. A very significant role.
   - ☐ B. A rather significant role.
   - ☐ C. Somewhat influential, but not a major role.
   - ☐ D. A relatively minor role.
   - ☐ E. No role at all.

8. To what extent do you believe in a life after death?
   - ☐ A. Strongly believe in it.
   - ☐ B. Tend to believe in it.
   - ☐ C. Uncertain.
   - ☐ D. Tend to doubt it.
   - ☐ E. Convinced it does not exist.

9. Regardless of your belief about life after death, what is your wish about it?
   - ☐ A. I strongly wish there were a life after death.
   - ☐ B. I am indifferent as to whether there is a life after death.

C. I definitely prefer that there
not be a life after death.

10. To what extent do you believe in
reincarnation?
A. Strongly believe in it.
B. Tend to believe in it.
C. Uncertain.
D. Tend to doubt it.
E. Convinced it cannot occur.

11. How often do you think about
your own death?
A. Very frequently (at least once
a day).
B. Frequently.
C. Occasionally.
D. Rarely (no more than once a
year).
E. Very rarely or never.

12. If you could choose, when would
you die?
A. In youth.
B. In the middle prime of life.
C. Just after the prime of life.
D. In old age.

13. When do you believe that, in
fact, you will die?
A. In youth.
B. In the middle prime of life.
C. Just after the prime of life.
D. In old age.

14. Has there been a time in your life
when you wanted to die?
A. Yes, mainly because of great
physical pain.
B. Yes, mainly because of great
emotional upset.
C. Yes, mainly to escape an in-
tolerable social or interper-
sonal situation.
D. Yes, mainly because of great
embarrassment.
E. Yes, for a reason other than
above.
F. No.

15. What does death mean to you?
A. The end; the final process of
life.
B. The beginning of a life after
death; a transition, a new
beginning.
C. A joining of the spirit with a
universal cosmic consciousness.
D. A kind of endless sleep; rest
and peace.
E. Termination of this life but
with survival of the spirit.

F. Don't know.
G. Other (specify):_____

16. What aspect of your own death is
the most distasteful to you?
A. I could no longer have any
experiences.
B. I am afraid of what might happen to my body after death.
C. I am uncertain as to what
might happen to me if there is
a life after death.
D. I could no longer provide for
my dependents.
E. It would cause grief to my relatives and friends.
F. All my plans and projects
would come to an end.
G. The process of dying might be
painful.
H. Other (specify):_____

17. How do you feel today?
A. On top of the world.
B. Wonderful.
C. Cheerful.
D. On the whole, all right.
E. About like the average person.
F. Just fair.
G. Kind of low.
H. Down and out.
I. Wish I were dead.

18. How do you rate your present
physical health?
A. Excellent.
B. Very good.
C. Moderately good.
D. Moderately poor.
E. Extremely bad.

19. How do you rate your present
mental health?
A. Excellent.
B. Very good.
C. Moderately good.
D. Moderately poor.
E. Extremely bad.

20. Based on your present feelings,
what is the probability of your
taking your own life in the near
future?
A. Extremely high (I feel very
much like killing myself).
B. Moderately high.
C. Between high and low.
D. Moderately low.
E. Extremely low (very improb-
able that I would kill myself).

21. In your opinion, at what age are
people most afraid of death?

A. Up to 12 years.
B. Thriteen to 19 years.
C. Twenty to 29 years.
D. Thirty to 39 years.
E. Forty to 49 years.
F. Fifty to 59 years.
G. Sixty to 69 years.
H. Seventy years and over.

22. What is your belief about the
causes of *most* deaths?
A. Most deaths result directly
from the conscious efforts by
the persons who die.
B. Most deaths have strong com-
ponents of conscious or un-
conscious participation by the
persons who die (in their
habits and use, misuse, non-
use or abuse of drugs, alcohol,
medicine, etc.).
C. Most deaths just happen; they
are caused by events over
which individuals have no
control.
D. Other (specify):_____

23. To what extent do you believe
that psychological factors can in-
fluence (or even cause) death?
A. I firmly believe that they can.
B. I tend to believe that they can.
C. I am undecided or don't know.
D. I doubt that they can.

24. When you think of your own
death (or when circumstances
make you realize your own mor-
tality), how do you feel?
A. Fearful.
B. Discouraged.
C. Depressed.
D. Purposeless.
E. Resolved, in relation to life.
F. Pleasure, in being alive.
G. Other (specify):_____

25. What is your present orientation
to your own death?
A. Death-seeker.
B. Death-hastener.
C. Death-accepter.
D. Death-welcomer.
E. Death-postponer.
F. Death-fearer.

26. How often have you been in a
situation in which you seriously
thought you might die?
A. Many times.
B. Several times.
C. Once or twice.
D. Never.

27. To what extent are you interested in having your image survive after your own death through your children, books, good works, etc.?
- [ ] A. Very interested.
- [ ] B. Moderately interested.
- [ ] C. Somewhat interested.
- [ ] D. Not very interested.
- [ ] E. Totally uninterested.

28. For whom or what might you be willing to sacrifice your life?
- [ ] A. For a loved one.
- [ ] B. For an idea or a moral principle.
- [ ] C. In combat or a grave emergency where a life could be saved.
- [ ] D. Not for any reason.

29. If you had a choice, what kind of death would you prefer?
- [ ] A. Tragic, violent death.
- [ ] B. Sudden but not violent death.
- [ ] C. Quiet, dignified death.
- [ ] D. Death in line of duty.
- [ ] E. Death after a great achievement.
- [ ] F. Suicide.
- [ ] G. Homicidal victim.
- [ ] H. There is no "appropriate" kind of death.
- [ ] I. Other (specify):_____

30. Have your attitudes toward death ever been affected by narcotic or hallucinogenic drugs?
- [ ] A. Yes.
- [ ] B. I have taken drugs but my attitudes toward death have never been affected by them.
- [ ] C. I have never taken drugs.

31. If it were possible would you want to know the exact date on which you are going to die?
- [ ] A. Yes.
- [ ] B. No.

32. If your physician knew that you had a terminal disease and a limited time to live, would you want him to tell you?
- [ ] A. Yes.
- [ ] B. No.
- [ ] C. It would depend on the circumstances.

33. If you were told that you had a terminal disease and a limited time to live, how would you want to spend your time until you died?

- [ ] A. I would make a marked change in my life-style; satisfy hedonistic needs (travel, sex, drugs, other experiences).
- [ ] B. I would become more withdrawn; reading, contemplating or praying.
- [ ] C. I would shift from my own needs to a concern for others (family, friends).
- [ ] D. I would attempt to complete projects; tie up loose ends.
- [ ] E. I would make little or no change in my life-style.
- [ ] F. I would try to do one very important thing.
- [ ] G. I might consider committing suicide.
- [ ] H. I would do none of these.

34. How do you feel about having an autopsy done on your body?
- [ ] A. Approve.
- [ ] B. Don't care one way or the other.
- [ ] C. Disapprove.
- [ ] D. Strongly disapprove.

35. To what extent has the possibility of massive human destruction by nuclear war influenced your present attitudes toward death or life?
- [ ] A. Enormously.
- [ ] B. To a fairly large extent.
- [ ] C. Moderately.
- [ ] D. Somewhat.
- [ ] E. Very little.
- [ ] F. Not at all.

36. Which of the following has influenced your present attitudes toward your own death the most?
- [ ] A. Pollution of the environment.
- [ ] B. Domestic violence.
- [ ] C. Television.
- [ ] D. Wars.
- [ ] E. The possibility of nuclear war.
- [ ] F. Poverty.
- [ ] G. Existential philosophy.
- [ ] H. Changes in health conditions and mortality statistics.
- [ ] I. Other (specify):_____

37. How often have you seriously contemplated committing suicide?
- [ ] A. Very often.
- [ ] B. Only once in a while.
- [ ] C. Very rarely.
- [ ] D. Never.

38. Have you ever actually attempted suicide?
- [ ] A. Yes, with an actual very high probability of death.
- [ ] B. Yes, with an actual moderate probability of death.
- [ ] C. Yes, with a actual low probability of death.
- [ ] D. No.

39. Whom have you known who has committed suicide?
- [ ] A. Member of immediate family.
- [ ] B. Other family member.
- [ ] C. Close friend.
- [ ] D. Acquaintance.
- [ ] E. No one.
- [ ] F. Other (specify):_____

40. How do you estimate your lifetime probability of committing suicide?
- [ ] A. I plan to do it some day.
- [ ] B. I hope that I do not, but I am afraid that I might.
- [ ] C. In certain circumstances, I might very well do it.
- [ ] D. I doubt that I would do it in any circumstances.
- [ ] E. I am sure that I would never do it.

41. Suppose that you were to commit suicide, what reason would most motivate you to do it?
- [ ] A. To get even or hurt someone.
- [ ] B. Fear of insanity.
- [ ] C. Physical illness or pain.
- [ ] D. Failure or disgrace.
- [ ] E. Loneliness or abandonment.
- [ ] F. Death or loss of a loved one.
- [ ] G. Family strife.
- [ ] H. Atomic war.
- [ ] I. Other (specify):_____

42. Suppose you were to commit suicide, what method would you be most likely to use?
- [ ] A. Barbiturates or pills.
- [ ] B. Gunshot.
- [ ] C. Hanging.
- [ ] D. Drowning.
- [ ] E. Jumping.
- [ ] F. Cutting or stabbing.
- [ ] G. Carbon monoxide.
- [ ] H. Other (specify):_____

43. Suppose you were ever to commit suicide, would you leave a suicide note?
- [ ] A. Yes.
- [ ] B. No.

44. To what extent do you believe that suicide should be prevented?
- [ ] A. In every case.
- [ ] B. In all but a few cases.
- [ ] C. In some cases, yes; in others, no.
- [ ] D. In no case; if a person wants to commit suicide society has no right to stop him.

45. What efforts do you believe ought to be made to keep a seriously ill person alive?
- [ ] A. All possible effort: transplantations, kidney dialysis, etc.
- [ ] B. Efforts that are reasonable for that person's age, physical condition, mental condition, and pain.
- [ ] C. After reasonable care has been given, a person ought to be permitted to die a natural death.
- [ ] D. A senile person should not be kept alive by elaborate artificial means.

46. If or when you are married would you prefer to outlive your spouse?
- [ ] A. Yes; I would prefer to die second and outlive my spouse.
- [ ] B. No; I would rather die first and have my spouse outlive me.
- [ ] C. Undecided or don't know.

47. What is your primary reason for the answer which you gave for the question above?
- [ ] A. To spare my spouse loneliness.
- [ ] B. To avoid loneliness for myself.
- [ ] C. To spare my spouse grief.
- [ ] D. To avoid grief for myself.
- [ ] E. Because the surviving spouse could cope better with grief or loneliness.
- [ ] F. To live as long as possible.
- [ ] G. None of the above.
- [ ] H. Other (specify): _____

48. How important do you believe mourning and grief rituals (such as wakes and funerals) are for the survivors?
- [ ] A. Extremely important.
- [ ] B. Somewhat important.
- [ ] C. Undecided or don't know.
- [ ] D. Not very important.
- [ ] E. Not important at all.

49. If it were entirely up to you, how would you like to have your body disposed of after you have died?
- [ ] A. Burial.
- [ ] B. Cremation.
- [ ] C. Donation to medical school or science.
- [ ] D. I am indifferent.

50. Would you be willing to donate your heart for transplantation (after you die)?
- [ ] A. Yes, to anyone.
- [ ] B. Yes, but only to a relative or a friend.
- [ ] C. I have a strong feeling against it.
- [ ] D. No.

51. What kind of a funeral would you prefer?
- [ ] A. Formal, as large as possible.
- [ ] B. Small, relatives and close friends only.
- [ ] C. Whatever my survivors want.
- [ ] D. None.

52. How do you feel about "lying in state" in an open casket at your funeral?
- [ ] A. Approve.
- [ ] B. Don't care one way or the other.
- [ ] C. Disapprove.
- [ ] D. Strongly disapprove.

53. What is your opinion about the costs of funerals in the U.S. today?
- [ ] A. Very much overpriced.
- [ ] B. No one has to pay for what he doesn't want.
- [ ] C. In terms of costs and services rendered, prices are not unreasonable.

54. In your opinion, what would be a reasonable price for a funeral?
- [ ] A. Under $300.
- [ ] B. From $300 to $600.
- [ ] C. From $600 to $900.
- [ ] D. From $900 to $1,500.
- [ ] E. More than $1,500.

55. What are your thoughts about leaving a will?
- [ ] A. I have already made one.
- [ ] B. I have not made a will, but intend to do so some day.
- [ ] C. I am uncertain or undecided.
- [ ] D. I probably will not make one.
- [ ] E. I definitely won't leave a will.

56. To what extent do you believe in life insurance to benefit your survivors?
- [ ] A. Strongly believe in it; have insurance.
- [ ] B. Tend to believe in it; have or plan to get insurance.
- [ ] C. Undecided.
- [ ] D. Tend not to believe in it.
- [ ] E. Definitely do not believe in it; do not have and do not plan to get insurance.

57. Assuming that there has been an increase in the amount of concern with death in the U.S. in the last 25 or 50 years, to what principally do you attribute this change?
- [ ] A. Wars.
- [ ] B. Domestic violence.
- [ ] C. Pollution of the environment.
- [ ] D. Atomic and nuclear bombs.
- [ ] E. Existential philosophy.
- [ ] F. The drug culture.
- [ ] G. Television.
- [ ] H. No change.
- [ ] I. Other (specify): _____

In order to evaluate this survey it is important to know a few things about the background of each person who responds. Please help by answering these questions.

58. What is your sex?
- [ ] A. Male.
- [ ] B. Female.

59. What is your age?
- [ ] A. Under 20.
- [ ] B. From 20 to 24.
- [ ] C. From 25 to 29.
- [ ] D. From 30 to 34.
- [ ] E. From 35 to 39.
- [ ] F. From 40 to 49.
- [ ] G. From 50 to 59.
- [ ] H. From 60 to 64.
- [ ] I. Sixty-five or over.

60. How many brothers and sisters do you have?
- [ ] A. One.
- [ ] B. Two.
- [ ] C. Three.
- [ ] D. Four.
- [ ] E. Five.
- [ ] F. Six or more.
- [ ] G. None; I was an only child.

61. To what racial group do you belong?
- [ ] A. Caucasian.
- [ ] B. Negro.
- [ ] C. Oriental.
- [ ] D. Other.

62. What is your marital status?
- [ ] A. Single.
- [ ] B. Married once.

☐ C. Remarried.
☐ D. Separated.
☐ E. Divorced.
☐ F. Living with someone.
☐ G. Widow.
☐ H. Widower.

63. What is your religious background?
☐ A. Protestant.
☐ B. Roman Catholic.
☐ C. Jewish.
☐ D. Other.

64. How religious do you consider yourself to be?
☐ A. Very religious.
☐ B. Somewhat religious.
☐ C. Slightly religious.
☐ D. Not at all religious.
☐ E. Antireligious.

65. What is your political preference?
☐ A. Republican.
☐ B. Independent.
☐ C. Democratic.
☐ D. Other.

66. Would you describe your political views?
☐ A. Very liberal.
☐ B. Somewhat liberal.
☐ C. Moderate.
☐ D. Somewhat conservative.
☐ E. Very conservative.

67. What is your level of education?
☐ A. Grade school.
☐ B. High-school graduate.
☐ C. Some college.
☐ D. College graduate.

☐ E. Some graduate school.
☐ F. Master's degree.
☐ G. Ph.D., M.D. or other advanced degree.

68. What is the approximate annual income of your family?
☐ A. Less than $5,000.
☐ B. From $5,000 to $10,000.
☐ C. From $10,000 to $15,000.
☐ D. From $15,000 to $25,000.
☐ E. From $25,000 to $50,000.
☐ F. More than $50,000.

69. What area of the country would you call your home?
☐ A. West.
☐ B. Southwest and mountain states.
☐ C. Midwest.
☐ D. South.
☐ E. New England.
☐ F. Middle Atlantic.
☐ G. Other than U.S.

70. What is the population of the city or community you live in?
☐ A. Under 10,000.
☐ B. From 10,000 to 50,000.
☐ C. From 50,000 to 100,000.
☐ D. From 100,000 to 500,000.
☐ E. From 500,000 to 1,000,000.
☐ F. Over 1,000,000.

71. What are your present living arrangements?
☐ A. With my family.
☐ B. In a dormitory, shared dwelling or apartment with others.
☐ C. Living alone (in room, apartment or house).

72. What is your present occupation?
☐ A. Student.
☐ B. Elementary or H.S. teacher.
☐ C. Housewife.
☐ D. White-collar, clerical or sales.
☐ E. Technician, craftsman, etc.
☐ F. College professor or instructor.
☐ G. Business manager or executive.
☐ H. Unemployed.
☐ I. Other.

73. Do you work professionally as one of the following?
☐ A. Physician.
☐ B. Psychologist.
☐ C. Guidance counselor.
☐ D. Social worker.
☐ E. Lawyer.
☐ F. Engineer or scientist.
☐ G. Clergyman.
☐ H. None of the above.

74. If you have completed one or more of the previous *Psychology Today* questionnaires on
Cities,
Law,
Drugs, or Sex,
please indicate which ones: _____

_____

75. What effect has this questionnaire had on you?
☐ A. It has made me somewhat anxious or upset.
☐ B. It has made me think about my own death.
☐ C. It has reminded me how fragile and precious life is.
☐ D. No effect at all.
☐ E. Other effects (specify):

_____

Bibliography

Bensley, Loren B., Jr. *Death Education as a Learning Experience*. Washington, DC: ERIC Clearinghouse on Teacher Education, 1975. ERIC Document ED 115 580.
The 24-page brochure provides the user with a definition of death education, a basic philosophy, and a list of points to be taken into consideration when planning a unit or course. Intended as a guide for teachers of high school students. The bibliography, although dated, is useful. Available from the clearinghouse for 55 cents each.

Bernstein, Joanne E. *Books to Help Children Cope with Separation and Loss*. 2d ed. New York: Bowker, 1983.
Divided into two parts: the first contains essays on research and current developments dealing with death, divorce, illness, and adoption; the second is a subject-arranged, annotated bibliography of books on these topics.

Best, Gary A. *Death Education: The Special Education Teacher's Role*. Paper presented at the World Congress on the Future of Special Education, Stirling, Scotland. June 25–July 1, 1978. 5 pp. ERIC Document ED 158 522.
Discusses the significant role the teacher plays in the living process of the dying child. Considers the teacher's need for support in dealing with mourning and grief.

Death Education: Pedagogy, Counseling, Care—An International Quarterly. Hannelore Wass, ed. Hemisphere Publishing Corporation, 1025 Vermont Ave., NW, Washington, DC 20005.
A periodical devoted entirely to the topic of death education and all related issues. In addition to the articles on death and dying, reviews are included on current print and nonprint materials.

Eason, William M. *The Dying Child: The Management of the Child or Adolescent Who Is Dying*. Springfield, IL: Charles C. Thomas, 1981.
Author deals with practical day-to-day realities of the dying child and how to best manage these predictable problems. Discussion is also given to the effects this process has on the dying child's family.

Essence: Issues in the Study of Aging, Dying and Death. Stephen Fleming and Richard Lonetto, eds. Atkinson College Press, 4700 Keele St., Downsview, ON, Canada. Quarterly.
A Canadian periodical that takes an issues approach to the topic of dying, death, and the process of aging. Book reviews are occasionally included.

Fassler, Joan. *Helping Children Cope*. New York: Macmillan, 1978.
Of the four chapters devoted to stress-related topics which children might encounter, the first discusses death. A brief, selective bibliography concludes the chapter.

Fruehling, James A., ed. *Sourcebook on Death and Dying*. 1st ed. Chicago: Marquis Professional Publications, 1982.
A compendium of previously published articles and statistical information arranged in three parts: "Current Issues," "Facts and Figures," and "Sources of Information and Assistance." Directory information is provided for associations, hospices, memorial societies, and self-help groups.

Goldstein, Eleanor C. "Death & Dying." *Social Issues Resources Series*. Vols. 1–2. Boca Raton, FL: Social Issues Resources Series, Inc., 1982–1983.
Includes a broad spectrum of reprinted articles from popular magazines on the subject of death awareness.

Gordon, Audrey K. and Klass, Dennis. *They Need to Know: How to Teach Children about Death*. Englewood Cliffs, NJ: Prentice-Hall, 1979.
The book is divided into two parts: "The Child's Experience of Death" and "Teaching about Death." Two excellent chapters deal specifically with "Coping with Death and Dying in the School Setting" and "Suggested Curricula by Grade and Goal." Nine appendices conclude the monograph.

Gyulay, Jo-Eileen. *The Dying Child*. New York: McGraw-Hill, 1978.
Based on experiences of a pediatric nurse, the author approaches the subject from a caring point of view, not only for

the dying child but also for the family and friends who must assist and deal with the inevitable.

Knowles, Donald W. and Reeves, Nancy. *But Won't Granny Need Her Socks?* Dubuque, IA: Kendall/Hunt, 1983.
The book is based on the authors' observation, research, and personal experience conducting a series of counseling workshops on the topic of dealing effectively with children's concerns about death and dying. Guidelines and activities for commonly asked questions by children are discussed. Important resources conclude the workbook.

Kübler-Ross, Elisabeth. *On Death and Dying*. New York: Macmillan, 1969.
In this classic monograph, the author discusses her encounters and insights about dealing with dying patients and what they have to offer the living about their and our own finality.

Kübler-Ross, Elisabeth, ed. *Death: The Final Stage of Growth*. Englewood Cliffs, NJ: Prentice-Hall, 1975.
A collection of writings by young and older authors of varying professional backgrounds and religions that concern the meaning of life and thoughts on death. The book is a proclamation of life to be lived to its fullest with death being nothing more than a part of the continued growth process.

Martinson, Ida Marie, ed. *Home Care for the Dying Child: Professional and Family Perspectives*. New York: Appleton-Century-Crofts, 1976.
A compilation of articles covering the professional health services available for the dying child and preparations provided by nurses and doctors for the family in dealing with terminal illness.

Mills, Gretchen C., et al. *Discussing Death: A Guide to Death Education*. Homewood, IL: ETC Publications, 1976.
A curriculum guide of activity ideas to motivate students in a classroom setting to discuss concepts relating to death. Divided into levels beginning with five- to six-year-olds and continuing through the young adult years. Each level contains selected resources for further investigation.

Mitchell, Marjorie E. *The Child's Attitude toward Death*. New York: Schocken Books, 1967.
Takes a problematic approach by exploring individuals' religious, scientific, and sociological backgrounds and how these determine reactions and ideas about death. Examines related fears held by children and adolescents and presents ways to manage these attitudes.

Ogg, Elizabeth. *A Death in the Family*. New York: Public Affairs Committee, 1976.
A pamphlet that provides the user with a straightforward and brief overview of the "Typical Phases of Grief," "Extreme Reactions," "Children and Death," and "Finding the Thread of Continuity."

"On Death." Community Services, Greenwich Public Library, 101 Putnam Ave., Greenwich, CT 06830.
A book list for librarians considering publicity and programing in this area. Available free upon request.

Prince, Arlene, comp. *Death and Dying: A Mediagraphy*. Seattle, WA: University of Washington and Allied Memorial Council, 1977.
Although the mediagraphy is somewhat dated, this is the most comprehensive volume on available software about this topic. The compiler/editor has included sections on media both reviewed and unreviewed including films, videotapes, filmstrips, and audiotapes/records. Indexes by title, subject, and distributor are also provided.

Rosenthal, Nina Ribak. "Teaching Educators to Deal with Death." *Death Education* 2 (1978): 293–306.
An overview of a seminar on death education for teachers is described. Evaluations by the participants of activities undertaken are included.

Russell, Robert D. and Purdy, Candace O. *Coping with Death and Dying*. Glenview, IL: Scott, Foresman, 1980.
Written primarily for the young adult reader who wishes to explore the topic independently or in a classroom setting, the book provides the user with facts, questions, and activities for exploration of feelings and attitudes toward the process. Other books to read conclude each of the chapters.

Sahler, Olle Jane Z., ed. *The Child and Death*. Saint Louis, MO: The C. V. Mosby Co., 1978.
A two-and-a-half day symposium by the same title makes up the major content of the book. Divided into four sections, topics covered include the fatally ill child, the caregiver, survivorship, and ethical and educational considerations.

"Selected Books and Pamphlets on Chronic Illness and Handicaps." Association for the Care of Children's Health, 3615 Wisconsin Ave., NW, Washington, DC 20016.
A bibliography including books, pamphlets, and government publications. A listing with addresses of clearinghouses is also provided. Available free from ACCH.

Sharapan, Hedda. " 'Mister Rogers' Neighborhood': Dealing with Death on a Children's Television Series," *Death Education* 1 (1977): 131–36.
Article details primary considerations in producing segments on death education for this series. Includes selected dialog from the programs and reactions from viewers.

Stanford, Gene. "A Mini-Course on Death," *Scholastic Teacher* (September 1973): 40–44.
Reviews numerous media appropriate for a course on death and then relates possible approaches for teaching the topic in a high school setting.

"Understanding Death & Dying: A Book List of Helpful Reading for Children." Compiled by Rockland County Public Library and Ramapo Catskill Library System, n.d.
The bibliography is divided into five sections: picture books, books for younger readers, books for intermediate readers, books for older readers, and nonfiction. Single copies of the pamphlet are available free by writing to the Ramapo Catskill Library System, 619 North St., Middleton, NY 10940. A self-addressed, stamped envelope must be included with the request.

Wass, Hannelore, ed. *Dying: Facing the Facts*. New York: Hemisphere, 1979.
The editor has divided the 15-chapter monograph into three parts: "The Problem: Denial and Ambivalence toward Death," "The Data: The Facts of Death," and "The Challenge: Meeting the Issues." Two chapters are particularly relevant for parent/teacher reference: "Children and Death" and "Death Education for All." Additional print and nonprint resources are suggested at the end of each chapter.

Wass, Hannelore and Corr, Charles A., eds. *Childhood and Death*. New York: Hemisphere, 1983.
A comprehensive compilation of writings by authorities on death education for children. An annotated bibliography concludes the monograph.

————. *Helping Children Cope with Death: Guidelines and Resources*. New York: Hemisphere, 1982.
Provides a summary of the ways that death education for children can be accomplished. Contains an annotated bibliography of books and nonprint appropriate for use with children.

Wass, Hennelore; Corr, Charles; Pacholski, Richard A.; and Sanders, Catherine M. *Death Education: An Annotated Resource Guide II*. New York: Hemisphere, 1983.
Provide the user with a comprehensive inventory of available media resources on this topic. Topical index provides access to specific entries.

Watts, Richard G. *Straight Talk about Death with Young People*. Philadelphia, PA: Westminster Press, 1975.
Written as a result of the author's experiences with junior high school age young adults, the book is structured by questions most commonly asked by this group with realistic, straightforward facts as answers. Could be useful as a text or reference.

Zeligs, Rose. *Children's Experience with Death*. Springfield, IL: Charles C. Thomas, 1974.
Written from the point of view of a psychologist, this book discusses the need for informing children about this natural process prior to the actual experience. How to deal with questions from a child who is dying is also discussed.

Index

Compiled by Linda Webster